By Anita Sullivan

Nonfiction

The Seventh Dragon: The Riddle of Equal Temperament
The Family Piano (Essays from NPR)

Poems

Nutritious Desserts
The Middle Window

Ikaria

A Love Odyssey on a Greek Island

*Oh, my heart, how can you
my heart how, my heart how can you endure
in the midst of so much love and so much beauty?*

Mikis Theodorakis (lyrics from "My April")

by

Anita Sullivan

Burning Daylight, an imprint of
Pearn and Associates, Inc.
Colorado

Copyright © 2008 by Anita Sullivan. All rights reserved.

Published by Burning Daylight, an imprint of Pearn & Associates, Inc., Boulder, Colorado. For general information about our other products and services, please contact us at happypoet@hotmail.com (720) 406-8858.

Cover design by Anne Kilgore.

Acknowledgements:
Following is a list of magazines where some chapters in this volume first appeared as essays: "Living on an Island" in *Grand Tour*, Summer 1996; "Jasmine" in *Northwest Review*, Fall, 1998; "Moni Mounte" in *Brother Jonathan Review*, Winter 2000; "Living on an Island" in *Greece in Print*, July/August 2005.

Translations of poems by George Seferis are by the author.

Limit of Liability/Disclaimer of Warranty: While the publisher and the author have used their best efforts in preparing this book, they make no representations or warranties with respect to accuracy or completeness of the contents of this book and specifically disclaim any implied warranties. Neither publisher nor the author shall be liable for any loss of profit or any other commercial damages, including but not limited to special, incidental, consequential, or other damages.

Library of Congress Control Number: 2008924323

Sullivan, Anita 1942
Ikaria, by Anita Sullivan. First Edition.
ISBN 978-0-9777318-6-2 paperback

for Quiet, her wild heart

CONTENTS

First Time to Greece / 1

Living on an Island / 8

The Violin / 19

The Language / 25

Getting Around / 34

Deciding to Go / 42

The Gardens / 48

Having a Coffee /55

Wilderness / 60

The Naming of Things / 66

Moni Mounté / 71

Bathing / 78

Life Beautiful / 86

Jasmine / 94

Merely Voice / 101

Honey and Wine / 107

Epilogue / 118

Biography / 121

Ikaria

First Time to Greece

*Now that we can travel anywhere
we need no longer take the poets
and myth-makers for sure witnesses
about disputed facts.*
         Heraclitos

Because I am afraid to come to Greece for the first time totally alone, I start off with a two-week tour. I have a bad attitude about tours, but this one promises to explore "herbs and plants on some of the lesser known Greek islands." *Lesser known* sounds even more appealing than the plants.

I have a great need to be silent. I am recovering from a lost love. During the six months before this trip, I fell in love with a Crete-born graduate student who was earning a little extra money teaching his native language. I feel very foolish to find myself now as emotionally devastated as if I were 20 and had just discovered for the first time that unbridled passion for someone doesn't turn him into a soul mate. My brief relationship with Mikis was not a love affair at all, only the confusing of affection for a new language with affection for the person who was transmitting it; and the wistful exaggerations of a middle-aged romantic confronted with what in Greece they call "the Cretan glance." I wish now I didn't have to speak for a year, but could live only through my eyes and ears, filling myself as if I were a doll getting a whole new batch of stuffing.

On the bus I spend much time looking out the window, listening to the backgammon game going on a few seats behind me, listening to a passenger carry on a conversation in spurts and giggles with the bus driver, who speaks no English. The voices drift around me. The passions which have been propelling me towards Greece for half a lifetime and particularly for the past six months have left me weak for anything but dumb observation. I can feel a growing excitement, because this place is at once totally different from anything I ever imagined, and at the same time as familiar as the cells of my body would be if they were suddenly magnified large enough for me to see. Though I had never seen them before, I would shout in recognition.

I think of Mikis every day. What actually happened between us over the past six months makes for a rather poor tale. Thus I will be effusive in my telling. Here we discover that he walks in a certain way: he ambles, he moves as if he were being pushed along slowly by a little wind, which does most of the work, so he can look around at the sky and the street and not bother to notice where his feet are going. He leans a little sideways in his brown leather jacket, and I can spot the rhythm of him ten blocks away: laconic, self-assured in the hips and shoulders—the unselfconscious motion—yet ambivalent in the way he speaks to the world. What is he thinking? He does not believe in God: a rational young scientist. And yet for Lent he gives up coffee and wine, two absolute lifelong essential liquids for any true Greek. Why?

He shrugs, and a quizzical gleam comes into his eyes. "No particular reason," he says. "I am not religious," he adds to Steve (the other student), who doesn't understand why anyone would give up something for Lent unless motivated by a true belief. But I used to be a Catholic, and I remember the joy of small ascetic acts, self-imposed in secret. "You're drinking peppermint tea!" I had exclaimed when we all sat down, so he felt obliged to tell us why not the usual coffee. And I discovered someone else in the world who would give up something for Lent without even being a Christian.

Ikaria

Coming in to Athens on the plane was a silent process. I looked down at the light brown shapes of the islands and kept realizing that turquoise stuff between them actually was the Mediterranean. It's almost frightening to be plunged abruptly into this world that seems to consist of villages and sea. Like Alice-in-Wonderland I can feel many familiar shapes and sizes dwindling away, and what is left I do not know how to comprehend. Cees Nooteboom, the Dutch travel writer said, "If we had less information things would be more complicated in a more essential way." Suddenly I feel bereft of information.

In the village of Delfi, after a five-hour bus ride, I walk out early in the morning past a patient brown donkey tethered to an almond tree and pick an olive sprig to press between the pages of my book of George Seferis' poems. I chose to bring this heavy hardback along on my trip because Mikis introduced the Nobel Prize winner as one of his favorite poets. The poems are delicate, subtle, deep . . . . Surely anyone who loves such poetry must have a magnificent soul. I cherish the poems as an indissoluble connection between us.

Here in Delfi I am pleased to recognize, prior to instruction, many flowers and plants from my childhood in Southern California: olives, oleander, bougainvillea, hibiscus, jasmine. And here grow the plane trees that Seferis wrote so much about, and that I now realize are the same as our sycamores. (*Now that you are leaving, take the child with you, the child who saw the light under that plane-tree.*) But where are all the other common species of trees one would expect to find in this climate? Surely a greater variety must have grown in Greece in ancient times. Maybe they were logged out centuries ago, to build ships for the Second Persian

Anita Sullivan

War? This is a question I will ask again and again each time I come to Greece, "What happened to the trees?" And I will keep getting different answers.

When we arrive on the island of Ikaria mid-way through the tour, I take an instant liking to the place, and decide to spend part of my free month here after the tour is over. This is a land I want to learn in the same slow and careful way I am coming to know the few acres surrounding my small apartment in Oregon.

On the first afternoon our whole group takes a leisurely three-mile walk along a dirt road high above the sea, from the village of Armenistis to the smaller village of Nas. Wild herbs in bloom cascade down the steep slopes. Our guide lectures as we walk. We note curry and wild peas, vetch, lavender, mullein, rumex, fennel, bamboo, rosemary, and something like our scotch broom with bright yellow blossoms. These are "screed," plants which grow in alkaline soil and in areas with very little dirt but many rocks. This northwest part of the island is like one huge rock garden, and the warm air is saturated with their scents. Each movement of my head brings a different mix of unfamiliar smells. Thus begins the root of memory: later in each of our lives these smells will have developed, by geometric progression deep inside our bodies, the power to knock each one of us flat with nostalgia. But now we can sniff in childlike abandon.

A few days later the eight of us pile into jeeps to drive up into the central mountains past the tree line, to a place dominated by huge boulders and slabs of stone, where only goats and hawks seem to live. Along the way we inch around hairpin turns through the fog into the village of Christos Raches, and keep driving till we come out into the sun again. The owners of the small jeep rental business have come along to guide us (after

Ikaria

prolonged negotiations by our tour leader over coffee in the hotel lobby). They are Ola and her husband Pericles with their daughter Rebecca, age five. Ola was born in Germany and came on holiday to Greece six years ago, met Pericles, and stayed. This is a common story here on Ikaria. Her husband has dark curly hair and enormous dark eyes. "You will meet many Greek men on your trip, and you will come back with an entirely different attitude about me," Mikis had said on the night before I left, as my faced burned with humiliation and fervor. I believed I would prove him wrong.

Homer used at least nine verbs to describe the actions of the human eye: you are "nailing" your eyes to something, you are "throwing" your eyes, you are sending out beams, you are gaping, you are protecting yourself from the Evil Eye, and you *are* somebody else's "eyes." According to Homer's anatomy, *seeing* was a very large experience, too important to be confined to two little balls in the upper part of the face. For example, you could also "see" with your lungs when you took a really deep breath. Your mind would be flooded with a vision—like windows in your chest!

The "Cretan Glance" is another variation of the supple and athletic uses of the sense of sight in Greece. It is simply a way that a man can look at a woman (not, I must add, the other way around), revealing to her in a blinding flash the power of his spirit. It is a kind of technique, I have come to believe, which rises naturally from the culture and would probably be difficult for a foreign male to learn. It happened to me one night as the three of us were sitting in the Beanery in Corvallis, Oregon, where we had our once-a-week lessons. There in the noise and bustle of this college coffee house we hunched around a small table with our steaming cups and did grammatical exercises, talked about Greece, translated the poetry of George Seferis as best we could at our very basic level of understanding. I looked up innocently from my book at a moment when Mikis happened to glance at me from his side of the table. But he actually *saw* me. That had never happened to me before, not in that lightning quick way that went clear down to my toes. It only takes about a second, but it must be a full second in order to work, and it was.

His eyes were the color of the changing sea, but I had not known that before. Like the sea, then, they changed. It was as if—using one of Homer's verbs—a beam had been across his eyes, and it moved aside. It moved aside and I could see *that he knew me.* Perhaps Odysseus felt something like this as he gazed into the whirlpool called Charybdis, which was about to drag his ship and his men to the very bottom of the sea. The whirlpool had pushed aside tons of sea water in its spinning, so that he could see a point miles down, a dry place in the earth's center. *But when she sucked the sea-water in, one might look right down through the swirling eddy while the rock roared hideously around her and the sea floor came to view, dark and sandy. Ashy terror seized on the crew.* This sounds like an exaggeration, a romantic fantasy, but it is not. I was looking at him and suddenly his eyes changed and it was as if he spoke with his eyes, saying, "Anita, yes, I am your soul, let that be a secret between us." How can anyone on earth resist something so powerful as being known?

Here in Ikaria I am totally unknown. My friends, parents, brother, two grown sons, I told them "I'm going to Greece for a couple of months." I don't carry a cell phone; I don't check my email, I have simply disappeared. After the first two weeks I will be a tourist without a tour. I have no guide books, no plans, only a map and a Greek dictionary, a book of poems by George

Ikaria

Seferis, my notebook, and very large hopes that are floating around like birds of prey, not knowing exactly where to alight. One of the women in the tour group says a word to Charlie, the owner of a bar in Armenistis, who rents out rooms on the top floor, and he tells her to let me know he will expect me in six days. I take this as a sign that things are working out, and I don't even ask how much he will charge for the room, which I have yet to set my eyes upon.

Anita Sullivan

Living on an Island

> *An island . . . is rimmed about with the eternal evidence of the contest between land and water, the unremitting siege of the sea, above which it rises untaken.*
> Paul Wilstach, *Islands of the Mediterranean*

I'm staying for two weeks in Armenistis, on the third floor of a restaurant and bar belonging to Charlie and Koula Fakaros and their son Yiannis who is one year older than my son Patrick. Every day I climb to my room on a white spiral staircase, as a princess would ascend to her tower. This building is one in a row of such establishments along the harbor in Armenistis, which has become—by default or design, I don't know—the chief tourist center on the island (even though the airport is clear at the other end, a good hour and a half by taxi). Despite being the designated island "tourist village," local Greeks outnumber foreigners, and the tourists strolling around the narrow streets have arrived after a long pilgrimage by plane, boat and taxi; they have not come in on cruise ships or big tourist buses.

The village's small hotels and pensions cater especially to European hiking groups. They walk the network of old footpaths, which used to be the only connection between the villages, until about the late 1960's when automobiles first came here to stay. Many of the roads up in the central mountain chain are still unpaved, full of switchbacks and deep ruts that challenge even the jeeps offered for rent at the car agencies, and especially the ubiquitous Fiat Pandas. Motorbikes are frequently nonplussed by the roads, and end up behaving like mere bicycles.

I came here at the end of my two-week tour, and more or less dropped myself off. I have adapted well to having nothing to do. I seem to be in a dormant state;

something behind my eyes is in suspension; I am sleeping a lot and not thinking sharply, not even seeing very well. It's still too cold for swimming in mid-May, I don't feel very ambitious to hike, there are no major archaeological sites to visit, and I have read most of the books I brought with me. All my energy is focused on forgetting a hopeless love and my entire body and spirit are responding with magnificent lassitude. In Greek, one verb for "forget" is λησμονώ (leezmo-no), which is dif- ferent from ordinary forgetting: it means "having the state of forgetfulness imposed on you from without." This happens, for example, when you drink of the River Lethe in Hades.

The protection of a mild soporific reverie allows, at last, the relaxation of the intense anguish I was living in for so many weeks just prior to this trip. Cautiously I can begin to think again.

I keep going over the facts of the case. There is no reason why Mikis should love me, and plenty of reasons why he should not. Mainly, I am fifty years old and he probably hasn't hit thirty yet. But he likes me. If he didn't, he would have broken off the Greek lessons as soon as he found out how I felt, as soon as I handed him that poem in the dark front seat of his car on a freezing February night.

"Oh, a poem in English?" he said. His voice always rose at the end of questions, with a kind of adolescent squeak that I found endearing. He started to open it.

"No! Read it later!" I gasped, and grabbed the door handle. A minute ago he had been musing aloud about going down to the Safeway for groceries at this late hour. Now I had re-shaped the whole course of his evening, maybe of his life. But I didn't speak, I only wrote.

Anita Sullivan

I remember standing breathlessly in my living room later that night, my heart pounding, wondering if he would call. Would he come to the door? I had written a love poem to a poor hapless foreign graduate student as if I were an eighteen-year-old, and I didn't even have sense enough to recognize how self-centered and offensive my action would probably seem. But this rash act was not arrogance on my part, only illness. I had become afflicted with what the ancient Greeks regarded as a disease—one that does not discriminate on the basis of age, sexual preference, previous experience or personal appearance, and for which there exists no prevention or cure—Eros.

I spread my books out on my large double bed, sit down cross-legged in front of them, and then stare out at the sea through the double doors, across the balcony. No rush. It seems very natural to move so slowly, as if all actions should always have a large cushion of inaction between them. "The one complaint I have about the Greek people is that we're lazy," says Yiannis (who, like many shopkeepers and restaurant owners in Greece, works seven days a week, 14 to 16 hours a day during tourist season). But the rhythm of the sea around an island demands a certain reciprocal speed of human action. Sometimes, lying in bed, I feel the whole island rocking.

On Sunday morning the day after I arrived, at a decent hour, I sat with Charlie drinking coffee and watching the Byzantine Sunday mass on television, from a cathedral in Athens. Charlie confessed that he watches it most Sundays, even though he doesn't particularly believe in the religion any more. Nobody else was around this early, Koula and Yiannis were in Athens, due to arrive home on the ferry later in the day.

Ikaria

I listened to the Byzantine chant and watched the elaborately-robed priests going through the Greek Orthodox ceremony, which I had never seen before. As the ceremony progressed, very static, not much busy work, it became clear that a very important element in the ritual is the Book. It was a large, beautifully ornamented Book resting on a lectern at the front of the cathedral. Priests took turns reading and chanting from it for quite a long time. Then it was carefully closed and carried in front of one of the priests as he walked slowly through the cathedral, in among the people who were sitting and standing around. The Grail, a major icon in pre-Roman Christian rituals and beliefs, was apparently a book first, before it took on its full complement of other symbolic guises: stone, cup . . . . Western Christianity reveres the Bible, of course, but does not seem to relish the outward manifestation of the Word in such an unabashedly tactile fashion as this.

Apparently having sized me up as a fellow heathen, Charlie interrupted our mesmerized TV watching with outbursts of opinion about religion. "It's bullshit!" he said, managing to say it in a way that did not sound vulgar, but as if it were the closest he could come in English to some infinitely more pointed Greek phrase. I told him how I was a fallen-away Catholic, and there we sat, side by side, sporadically reinforcing one another's views on the hypocrisy and inconsistencies in the practice of Eastern and Western Christianity, yet unable to tear ourselves away from the ritual being enacted on the screen in front of us. When I thought about it later, I realized how much fun it had been to talk about inconsistency while reveling in the practice of it. Drinking coffee, to boot.

Charlie is a shopkeeper, not a farmer, and he has his hands full during tourist season keeping his snack bar open into the wee hours of the morning. But he and Koula have a few acres of rocky hillside at the edge of the village. Here they keep a dozen goats, a dozen or so chickens and one magnificent male turkey. One day Charlie invited me up to watch him take care of these animals, and we drove a quarter of a mile in his van, parked beside the road and then half crawled straight up the side of the hill to the animal pens.

"You do this every day?" I asked, half an hour later when we got back into the van.

"Every goddamned day!" he said between his teeth, and then repeated himself, "Every goddamned day, twice a day, for nine years!"

Koula does not participate in this ritual. Charlie didn't tell me that, but I figured it out. The animals are the male responsibility. Twice a day either Charlie or Yiannis comes up here to untie the goats and lead them up the hill through the rocks for the choicest bits of forage, and later to lead them down again; to let the chickens out, round the chickens up again, and put them into their shack for the night; to look for eggs, to milk the goats. This cumbersome routine does provide some milk eggs and meat for the snack bar, but not enough to justify the expense and effort.

"I like them," Charlie shrugged, almost in wonder, while we drove a shorter distance back into the village than we had traveled with the goats up the mountainside. I think he is helplessly following the ancient Ikarian tradition of self-sufficiency, which the locals call "Αυταρκία" ("avtarkia," or autocracy). If you can live on vegetables from your small gardens, milk and meat from goats, honey from your bees, and the occasional delicacy of wild bird, you can behave like an autonomous nation. You don't need to depend on ships coming in; and if your island has no good harbors, even

Ikaria

the pirates will largely ignore you. Poverty has always been a price Ikarians are willing to pay for their independence. And Ikaria was actually an independent nation once for approximately five months in 1912 after expelling the last Turkish garrison. If it weren't for the Greek habit of total dependence on white bread—and the difficulty of raising wheat or other grains on the island (they tried it for awhile during the late 1940's, but it quickly wore out the soil)—it seems to me the Ikarians could, in fact, survive by themselves. They could if they wanted to. That's what Marilyn Monroe said in the film "Some Like it Hot," about her drinking problem: "I can stop drinking any time I want to; I just don't want to." So, how do you convince yourself you *want to* give up holding on to a hopeless infatuation? I keep writing letters to Mikis in my journal, and fighting to keep from mailing them.

Over the six-month period when the three of us were meeting for Greek lessons once a week, eight pieces of paper traveled from me to Mikis in some fashion. The very first one was about monkeys and typewriters.

It was January, New Years' weekend, and a foot of snow on the ground. Snow always makes me silly. I almost danced across the snow to our meeting that Tuesday, through the inside-out light that snow gives off at night. Somehow we got onto the question about how many monkeys on typewriters (computers) it would take to write the works of Shakespeare. I have thought about this a lot, in connection with the mathematics of permutations and combinations, as well as the nature of language. I think, truly, that it would never *happen, and for more than one reason. The most simple is that language never stops forming new iterations, and to get to the pattern of even a single soliloquy you would first have to come to the end of all possible word combinations. This in itself is not possible.*

So, Mikis and I, in true Socratic fashion, were "arguing" the question. Steve was listening. Sparks were flying between us, but it was nothing personal, we were actually after truth for about five glorious minutes. "But infinity is a long time." "Time has nothing to do with it. There is no guarantee that certain combinations would ever occur." "But the laws of permutations and combinations . . . ." We never reached agreement. I went home and spent an hour or two writing more about the subject, passionately wanting to convey to him something about language. He was a scientist, but obviously cared about poetry. Could I reach his heart through his mind? And, because there was snow on the ground (and thus I was feeling silly) I stuck the piece I had written into a plastic bag and taped it onto the door handle of his car. He didn't find it for three days, because like the rest of us, he was walking everywhere.

I wasn't in love with him then, but that single conversation probably made it inevitable. The next week, when I came into the Beanery, he looked up and said, with the sweet, formal courtesy he always showed towards me, "I got your note. I don't think I want to pursue it any further."

Unequivocal, yes? Wasn't he clearly signaling to me that I needed to back off? Very likely. But for Mikis there was never any such thing as an unequivocal statement. Always, radiating from his eyes, from his voice, from everything he said, was an ambivalence like the undertow in an ocean current, which caught me just as I was once again firmly heading for shore, and lifted me back up onto the waters. This ambivalence showed up constantly in the language exercises he gave us to translate every week, which he made up himself instead of cribbing them from a grammar book. Sentences like "Give me one reason not to go to Greece this summer, and I won't go;" *or* "Give me a kiss before you leave me;" *or* "I am so happy to be with you now." *Although by this time Mikis had likely sensed that his middle-aged student was falling prey to the Cretan glance, he was certainly not deliberately leading me on; he was simply sending out messages he did not know he was sending.*

I haven't talked with Koula very much. She spends her entire day behind the counter in the tiny kitchen of the bar, which is also the family kitchen and living room for them. She makes Greek coffee, omelets, pots of beans, goat-milk feta, and washes interminable loads of dishes. She is radiant as she does this, as if she were the saint of the kitchen.

Sometimes in the mornings, if I time it right, I can catch her just as she comes down the outdoor spiral metal stairs from the family rooms on the second floor. Unlike Charlie, she will serve me coffee and not sit down to drink a cup with me, but have her own cigarette and coffee behind the counter as she begins to work. We talk about our sons. She tells me Yiannis was a philosopher from the time he was a little boy, and I begin to understand what that means in Greece, where the men often seem to feel the need to act out a kind of Zorba-the-Greek persona, especially in front of female tourists. Yiannis doesn't do that, his philosophizing comes from a deeper place. Our conversation drifts, and settles for awhile on the cats. They have at least four adults, and one tiny, tiny white kitten, who is the only daughter of a very old female. This kitten delights the tourists, and probably attracts them to the bar with its innocent antics around the outdoor tables.

With an embarrassed blush Koula tells me the names of these animals; they come from American pop culture of the 50's. One of them is "Elvis," which she says was her idea. "Does the little one have a name yet?" I ask. "No!" she says firmly. "We have too many cats. My husband wants to keep her, but if we don't name her, then we won't keep her." I think of the grim fate of thousands of street cats all over Greece, who live off the pity of tourists in the summer, and then (so I have heard) die of starvation as soon as cold weather sets in. Watching the tiny kitten batting at its mother's tail, I think it would be neat to christen her. I don't tell Koula this, but later I say to Yiannis, "Before I leave Ikaria, I am going to name your kitten." He just grins.

Yiannis has become my friend. He is truly philosophical as his mother has wisely observed; he is willing to sit and wonder out loud about small things. Maybe this is one reason he has not yet married, since few people seem to have patience for this way of being. I come here and sit on the porch with him, looking out at the sea, and all the heavy confusions I am experiencing about Greek culture seem to be smoothed out, even if we don't say very much. Also, he is endlessly patient with my clumsy attempts to speak his language. We go back and forth from Greek to English.

Here I have met an old fisherman named Nikos who comes down from the mountain village of Christos Raches to drink ouzo in the evening at Charlie's bar. He wears an old grey sweater and dark slacks, even in the heat, and he has the weathered look of one who has worked all his life with his hands, around water. He talks to me in Greek, and I pretend to understand, then we clash our glasses together and shout "Yia mas!" and he says "Bravo!" He has promised to come and take me up the hill on the back of his motorbike one of these

Ikaria

days, to meet his wife and family. I have decided to stay on Ikaria an extra week, till May 27, to catch the "panigiri" or village dance, when Nikos will play island violin on the streets of Armenistis. "I am a musician first, a fisherman second," he says in Greek, and I can understand that.

Out of this trip I have a new attitude towards water. I have always said, "I am an air person, I am not a water person." But watching a fishing boat dozing its afternoon away at the dock, something half conscious in me thinks, "that rocking motion of the boat is *right*; it's what should always be happening to all of us; or, maybe it's what *is* happening, on a smaller scale, and we don't acknowledge it." We rock with the motion of the land, with the rhythm of the Earth and our own frenzied molecules. Since this is happening all the time, I would like to start noticing.

I went down to the sea at last and swam. I could have done so earlier, but I waited till it was really hot. The sea looks blue and green from above, but when you stand in the water you can see the sand and stones on the bottom, and your feet. I saw a small rowboat resting on the water as if it floated on air. "This is really just a great big lake, that's all it is," says Yiannis, waving his hand at the Mediterranean. And when the water is calm, just nibbling in swishes at the white sand, you do feel as if you are "inland" instead of on the "seashore."

An island exists by the grace of the sea, and in no other way; although they have long come, the two, to forget that old arrangement. But when you go up to the mountains on an island, a part of your mind remains behind as collateral to water—Theseus to the Cretans. You are always operating with that small part of you absent. In New Mexico and other inland deserts it is the opposite: that same part of your mind is set aside to be always aware of the *lack* of water. You live with a little burr of thirst just beneath your consciousness.

One afternoon when I was having lunch on the porch, reading, no other customers around, Yiannis was over by the door talking with a friend. A small airplane came into view on the horizon and Yiannis rushed over to the railing. He stood there silently watching for a solid minute or two, until it disappeared behind the village, and then turned to me with a slow grin. "This is what it's like, living on an island."

Ikaria

The Violin

> *He doesn't stop the strings; he licks the notes*
> (folk expression about traditional
> Greek fiddle playing)

One day in March when I was listening to Bach's "Coffee Cantata" in a downtown coffeehouse in Corvallis, I looked through its enormous windows to a group of people standing out on the sidewalk. They couldn't hear what was happening inside. It was winter. The trees had no leaves. The people stood around in their jackets talking, gesturing. They were in a different world; it could have been years ago, another country. Inside, the violins were playing precisely; we lifted our chins and held our jaws tight the way you do when you listen to Bach in intense happiness. Suddenly I noticed that the gestures of the people outside were in exact rhythm with the music. This went on for quite awhile. I wondered, "Is this how it has been all along?"

The fortieth day after Easter did come at last, and it was Festival day in Armenistis! In the morning a few men showed up down at the end of the street where it dead-ends into a parking lot. They washed the street and the harbor wall with sea water, making a huge noise and fuss with the generator, the large hoses, and their constant conversation. Then they whitewashed the harbor wall, end-to-end, across from the row of restaurants and shops. They brought in lots of table tops and planks for benches, and heaps of metal stands to hold them up and stacked them all down in the empty parking lot. After that the place quieted down and I sat around the bar for the rest of the afternoon writing and staring out at the sea. As Mikis used to say about the Greek tradition of men sitting one-to-a-table in the cafés, all facing the street without talking to each other and sipping coffee for hours: "They have their Doctor degrees in doing nothing."

About 8:00 p.m. a few hungry tourists strolled down to the end of the street to get some food at the "carry-out" in front of the mini-market, the traditional island "panigiri" (festival) meal consisting of broiled goat meat wrapped in waxed paper, two kinds of salad, bread, and island wine in small green bottles. The goats are free-ranging beasts, which don't belong to any one family but roam in the treeless land up in the mountains, among the boulders and wild vetch, and are basically up for grabs by locals. Anthropologically speaking, I guess you could say this is what's left to occupy the "hunter" component in their horticultural society, since they killed off all the deer, boar, and other edible mammals years ago.

I shunned the goat and supped on salad, bread and wine, after begging a little butter from Koula. The electricity went out for awhile at 9:00, but nobody paid any attention.

About 10:00 the musicians arrived and set up beside the mini-market, Nikos on the violin, assisted by a bouzouki and electric guitar. Sometimes there is a singer—though not tonight—or one of the smaller versions of the bouzouki. This typical island festival band represents a kind of nod in both directions: back towards the handmade folk instruments of the previous centuries, and forward towards the electronic age.

About 200 people had arrived from all over the island, and they sat at the picnic tables lined up and down the street, or up on the porches of the restaurants and bars. There was a dancing area at the end of the row of restaurants. Many of the dances were traditional, but every half hour or so they would play a free-for-all piece, and everyone, Greek and foreigner, could get up and respond randomly to the music. It was glorious to be jumping around like teenager, feeling manic energy animating your body. I want to take lessons and learn the Ikarian leaping dance, which keeps eluding me even when I haven't been sipping wine.

About 3:00 I went back to my room and tried to sleep, but I could hear Nikos still playing the mad violin music of the island. It is a controlled, wild, oriental kind of music, very traditional in basic rhythm and harmony, but violinists have their own energy, and the nature of the violin is to leap out. Sometimes it does go out and up, towards the ecstasy, just now and then, but you live for that.

At 6:00 I was leaning out my third-story window listening to the last strains of music. The sun was long up, and the sea was limpid in pink and pastel blue. After the violin finally quit I stayed at the window, feeling like Tennyson's Lady of Shalott who has turned away from her mirror forever. Down below, Yiannis walked slowly by on his way home. He looked up and grinned at me. "It's crazy, isn't it?" he said, shaking his head. "We dance all night long, and then we have to go to work in the morning. I don't know why we keep doing this, it's crazy!"

"I think it's just fine," I shrugged.

"Thank you for saying that!" he said with a broad smile, as if I had given him some genuine absolution. I shook my own head with a kind of motherly indulgence and went back to bed.

I am listening to Bach harpsichord and violin sonatas. The music is alien, so alien. It is squealing into the night, ridiculous, busy. The harpsichord is like the evening birds in the trees, making many small noises, *which come to you as many small noises; they never coalesce into a whole. This is like Zeno's fourth paradox.* Your body spreads out like a sail, wanting each one of those sounds.*

At 8:00 with memories of the last strains of Nikos' "violi" and the calm sunrise, I got dressed and went down to walk barefoot along the beach before breakfast. I went as far as the tiny church on its own little peninsula directly across the harbor from Armenistis. I see it every day from my third-story window. It was locked, but through the transom over the door I caught the glitter of colored window glass in its tiny dome, like marbles.

In mid-afternoon I came into the bar, blinking against the sudden darkness and there was Nikos, still in town. He had stopped by for a beer and a dozen or so cigarettes on his way back up the hill to Christos Raches, his home village. I told him how much I enjoyed his music and the dancing, and he showed me his swollen hands from playing for eight hours.

Then I said in Greek, "I used to play the violin." It was a pre-memorized sentence, one I had prepared for him a few days earlier, but not had a chance to use.

His face lit up, this old fisherman in grey sweater and dark slacks on a day of at least 80 degrees Fahrenheit, me in shorts, and he reached around behind his chair and lifted up his old black violin case with the rope attached so he can hang it around his neck while he rides his motor bike up the hill. He opened up the case, took out the violin and handed it to me.

I haven't touched a violin for 25 years, and I was never very good. I'm a piano tuner and music lover, but not a performer. Still, I tightened the bow and played a

G-major scale. It sounded surprisingly musical. Nikos was delighted.

After that, for an hour and a half or so we were handing the thing back and forth while he played some snatch of island music, and then I tried to play it too. I kept getting better, slowly. But the melodies are full of ornamentation and odd intonation patterns. Nikos told me, "You know music" (I could understand that in Greek). Yiannis was standing there watching us, and he translated sometimes when Nikos had something more complicated to say. I asked him who was going to play the violin after him, were his kids learning? He has six children, but none of them is interested in learning the fiddle. This is his father's instrument. He pointed out the worn spots by the chin rest and the neck. He says he taught himself to play, and he plays like a gypsy, with his eyes glowing. (I watched his profile last night as he leaned into his work.)

Since age 14 I have believed that there are musical instruments—and there is the violin. We had a piano in the house that nobody else played except me, because I was the only one willing to take lessons. One day in my early teens, as the designated musician in the family, I was offered the violin that had belonged to my great-uncle Fetti, a Hungarian aristocrat forced during the Depression to earn his living briefly, (so my grandmother assured me), as a piano tuner. After that, I never took piano lessons again.

When the violin arrived I was thrilled. The case was pock-marked, scratched, and the violin inside was a copy of an Amati, probably made in a factory in Germany. Only later when my ear became more refined, did I learn to admit that, yes, it was actually a pretty mediocre instrument. But this violin traveled with me to

Anita Sullivan

England, to New Zealand, to Virginia and ultimately to Oregon, where finally I loaned it to a public school music teacher who was gathering instruments for inner city kids in Portland. I knew I would never see it again. It is almost easier to admit you want to play the violin than it is to admit, finally, that you will not.

When Nikos and I were finally done, he put his violin back into its case and hung it around his neck, patting it affectionately and calling it his girlfriend. He stood up in his boots ready to make the trip up the hill. "You made me happy!" he said, shaking my hand. I promised to bring my violin with me next year. Maybe by then I'll find another one.

---

* Zeno's Fourth Paradox: If a bushel of corn turned out upon the floor makes a noise, each grain and each part of each grain must make a noise likewise; but, in fact, it is not so.

Ikaria

The Language

> *In Egypt the priests sing hymns to the Gods by uttering the seven vowels in succession, the sound of which produces as strong a musical impression on their hearers as if the flute and lyre were used . . . but perhaps I had better not enlarge on this theme.*
> Demetrius of Alexandria, 1st century B.C.E.

I have to address briefly the question, "Why do you keep coming back to Greece after your first trip, instead of going somewhere else instead?" The answer is simple: *the language*. That's where it started, and that's what still draws me year after year—a certain shaping of the air. But what about Mikis? And Eros?

When I say "the language" I mean something huge that includes the way Greeks move their bodies when they walk, and a certain beautiful hesitation of the tongue upon the S sounds in everyday speech that gives you a feeling that words are being cherished before they are released—fed—to the world (and to you, of course, waiting with your beak open). Mikis did all this as second nature, but for me it was brand new. Never before had I been confronted with the sheer physicality of language until I met Mikis and then, by extension, his country. We spend our lives becoming more vulnerable all the time, even as we harden ourselves by experience. The nature of poetry is to keep language alive by constantly refreshing it and subverting it—not letting it get stale with repetition. Greek, and then a single Greek man, and then Greece itself all landed on me at virtually the same time, like a huge poem.

In the Fall of my 50th year my friend Steve invited me to join him in a once-a-week tutoring session at a local coffee shop. After traveling to Greece for a couple of decades, he had just bought a house on the island of

Anita Sullivan

Paros, so he realized the time was overdue for him to learn the language. It would be easier if someone else were struggling along with him. I had never heard a word of Greek.

The first night, as we settled in with our coffee cups and our papers, I remember asking Mikis, "Do you have an infinitive in Greek?" (Is there infinity in Greek? Oh, yes, a dry infinity, lacking in the darker vowels, the wetter aspirants—a spare, a brittle, an inefficient infinity, the music of a plucked chordophone, infinitely subtle in its constant substitution of line for curve to catch shadow, not in a cusp but in a cistern.)
He gave me a calculating glance.
"Not exactly . . . . We don't have an infinitive like you do," he said slowly, and then proceeded to explain how "na" works, the little Greek word that seems to function just like the English "to" before a verb, but actually does not. It was an advanced place to begin a language, but we entered the labyrinth through that gate, and once it had happened that way—once Mikis said, "No, we don't have an infinitive, exactly," his mind was made up about how he was going to teach us, and we took our thread down with us through this particularly complex entry, which began to show side paths and turns and switchbacks immediately until soon we were entirely embroiled. There were easier ways, but we did not stop long enough at the beginning to consider them: the infinitive took us in.

Shortly after our first Greek lesson I drove to a large bookstore in Eugene near the University of Oregon to buy a Modern Greek grammar. I didn't find one, but I wandered back to the Classics section to look around.

Ikaria

Immediately I was plunged into an ecstasy of false scholarship; I was an Oxford student browsing in some old bookshop in London three centuries ago. Around me were people in dark cloaks, people who knew passages from Homer by memory, and thus held secrets of peculiarly powerful tones and rhythms inside their mouths. The light was dim, the bookshelves were very, very tall, blending into the black ceiling. Suddenly a young man appeared beside me. He saw the red book in my hand; I don't remember what it was.

"You are studying Greek?" he said.

"Just beginning," I murmured.

He took down another book from the section in front of us; it was a book of poems in ancient Greek. He opened the book and read aloud a couple of lines. The room was completely still, and the words fell into the stillness, making a sound I had never heard before. It was dry, thin, harsh. It didn't belong there.

I winced, almost embarrassed for the words. He closed the book, smiled, and vanished like the Cheshire cat, while the words he had whispered so quickly were still turning in the space beside me. And then, even if he hadn't pronounced the words exactly right: even if nobody, not even modern Greeks, knows what ancient Greek actually sounded like, the words I heard for just a few seconds were strange to me in a way that has tweaked my soul as if it were somebody's nose, and pulled it out of me into the air for a toss at the ceiling.

In speaking Modern Greek there are three parts to the way the words must come out to sound right, the lilt, the curl, and the stretch. First you pronounce it straight. That's like ordering up your hunk of granite, and your hammer and chisel. You pronounce it the way it tells you in the book, but then you must also sing it.

Your tongue has to be broken into parts as you speak. A good example is "kalimera," which means "good day." It's not a word, it is a small bird song.

Now I am in Athens near the end of my first two months in Greece. I am stuck here for an indefinite period because my passport and money and credit cards were all stolen out of my backpack while I was waiting for a bus in Omonia Square. Some quick-fingered person reached into the outside pocket and slipped them out. Ironically, I was on my way to the airport to meet Steve, who was arriving to spend his first summer in his new house on Paros. When I got there, he was surprised to see me, having completely forgotten extracting this promise from me two months before, when he had agreed to drive me to the airport at 4:00 in the morning for my big Greek trip. Not being a very noticing kind of guy, he failed on that occasion to observe that my eyes were red and hollow because I had been awake all night.

I had talked Mikis into meeting me for dinner at a local Mediterranean restaurant. He thought Steve would be coming too, but I told him the evening before that Steve had a conflict (a lie, since I had never invited him) and Mikis was courteous enough to let himself be caught in the trap. He arrived armed with a set of maps and guide books, and firmly refused my clumsy attempt to talk about a relationship. "Aren't you honored at all that an older woman, a poet, has fallen in love with you?" I said. This was the closest I ever got to simply saying aloud, "I love you," and it was my last attempt to introduce certainty into what still seemed to my deluded mind as ambivalence in his attitude. "Yes," he said, wrinkling his forehead in an attempt not to make a discourteous reply (to one of his elders), at which point, he turned to his maps and I knew the subject was closed. The final blow came near the end of our short meal when I innocently asked him if there was any message I might take with me to a member of his family, since he had been away from home for six years, and was not due to return until next Christmas. I wince now to see the expression of pain and polite distaste on his face, and to realize what an incredibly gauche error I had made with that question. Who was I to try to force myself into the intimate web of relationships that constituted his life as a Greek, an entire universe unknown to me? So, I staggered out of the restaurant in a blur of humiliation and despair, and literally walked the streets for hours, weeping, until exhaustion drove me home to finish packing. Never once did it occur to me to abort the trip.

Now, because Steve lightheartedly abandoned me (after loaning me $25) and went off to Paros on the ferry, I'm staying in a seedy hotel on credit and eating very sparsely with spare change, buying bags of peanuts and soft pretzels from the street vendors, drinking water from the hotel tap.

And because of this unexpected series of misfortunes it seems to me that "the whole thing" has come down on my head at last, this house of cards, this carefully constructed romantic notion about Greece—inspired by an even deeper romantic notion about the nature of true love. I have failed again. Sure, I have learned how to book hotel rooms, buy ferry tickets, get onto trains and buses, buy food, all in Greek and all by myself, a woman traveling alone. So, why do I feel as if I have failed, as if I continually fail minute by minute, every one of the 60-odd days I have spent in this country whose human beings are so full of grace? Of all the demons in me I most wished to leave behind and tiptoe away from (its seventy snake-heads lulled to sleep by bouzouki and violin) it was this one, my demon of small failure. And I have not. For now it seems to me that even my so-called successes were actually failures too, in that someone else would have done better. Someone else would have been able to play real music on the violin. Somebody else would have known some jokes or some silly games to play with toothpicks at the table on those days when Yiannis and his friends and I were sitting around drinking ouzo, instead of sit- ting quietly waiting for a chance to make a philoso- phical observation. I have not changed; I have not be- come a better person, a more assertive person; my old terror is still with me and I am afraid to go home.

More than that. Dumbly, irrationally, passion- ately, I want to stay here. A simple love of this place overpowers any other thoughts or feelings.

It is the language itself that has me pinned down like a donkey's tail to a corkboard. I cannot leave that sound. It is a ribbon in the air as I walk the streets. I receive it sensually, almost as if I were being stroked, or as if some internal massage, long withheld, were at last taking place. Oh, my cells, how they stretch and me- ander! I am quivering lightly in delight all day long— even today when I had to walk to the American Em- bassy, about two miles in the stifling heat, then down another mile and a half or so to the bank in Syntagma Square to find out that my travelers check reim- bursement money had not come in, then up to the hotel where they are letting me stay for free until I can re- cover all the stolen money and checks and credit cards. After that another visit to the O.T.E., the public tele- phone building to call Visa International on the "good phone," which I discovered by trial and error is phone #16. This has been a typical day for the last week.

Last night I went to the park again, near the hotel, where people take their nightly "volta," strolling up and down the pathways in the cool of the evening. A woman I was sitting next to on a park bench struck up a conversation. She was an elegant lady of about 65, wearing eye shadow and rouge and carrying a parasol. She was French, a widow, and had lived in Athens for many years. She told me her father was *such* a fine musician in Constantinople (not Istanbul), that the Byzantine Pope (the "Patera") gave him the equivalent of knighthood. Her brother was a general ("Now dead," she sniffed in dramatic sorrow). I suppose I was fortunate not to *comprend* too well or I would doubtless have heard in detail of the exploits and worth of many other members of her illustrious family. She had dark, expressive eyes and a patrician nose, was doubtless a real beauty when she was younger. I could understand French, but not speak it; I could speak Greek, but not understand it. On my next trip to Greece I will enroll in a language school, I promise myself.

The next day, again, my money has not arrived, but at least I do have a new passport (another walk in the stifling heat up to the Embassy). So, I will do the prudent, conservative thing, I will go to Olympic Airways to change my ticket. I console myself by endlessly recalculating the expenses I will save.

It takes about half an hour for the agent to change the ticket, mostly punching the computer keyboard and staring silently at it for long seconds, waiting. But as she is finally affixing the stamp to my ticket and as I turn around to walk to the cashier window on the other side of the room to pay the penalty, suddenly I can't do it. I simply cannot physically make it over to that window. It's as if I were about to abandon a child, or to carry out my first order as a soldier to shoot someone in the head. My body is refusing to move in obedience to a command which the mind has deemed logical and correct. Gilbert Murray says, in *Five Stages of Greek Religion*, "We read of judges in the seventeenth century who believed that witches ought to be burned and that the persons before them were witches, and yet would not burn them." I call this "body ethic," and bow mutely to its commands.

So, I turn back around and say, "I changed my mind!" and the Olympic agent takes the sticker off my ticket and says "No problem!" and I am staying five more days again. "You can't think in Greece!" says Pieter, the desk clerk at the hostel where I'm staying, a young man who came here from Holland a year ago on vacation and hasn't left yet. It's true.

The next morning my travelers check refund money is in. As a matter of fact, it was in yesterday, but they thought I had asked for a "transfer" instead of a "refund." Today, once again, I wait in a bank, fill out forms, sign my name over and over as the clock inches towards the 2:00 closing time and my stomach doesn't even bother to remind me that I've skipped breakfast and lunch again. I get away at last with $100.00 in drachmas, which means I'll go to Paros tomorrow on the ferry. With a bit of fire in my head.

On the ferry I glance at the 6:30 News on television where a sign-language interpreter is working beside the main newscaster. I do a double take, because her hands are moving at such a leisurely pace I first assume she must be there for some other reason. Although Greeks talk lickety-split just like everybody else

Ikaria

in the world, apparently they still can't make up for the massive number of syllables in their gorgeous language. Thus, (I reason), meaning must happen much more slowly in Greek than in English. With this thought I relax into my seat and fall asleep.

Anita Sullivan

Getting Around

Now I am wanting a little quiet,
let there be a hut for me on a hillside
or near a seashore
let there be a blued sheet at my window
spread like the sea...
The evening will fall,
flocks of sheep with echoing bells
will come down to their folds
like a simple thought
and I will lie down to sleep
because I will not have even a candle
to read by.
George Seferis

Places to sit. We tourists move from one to another. SIT at a table under an umbrella in front of a taverna inside the sea wall. SET your pepper shaker inside the bread basket to keep it from blowing away in the wind; feel the sun on your neck, watch an old Greek couple wade hand in hand into the sea (nobody else is swimming today). Will they survive?

Doorways will do. If you are too broke even to SIT at a table and order a frappe (iced coffee), you might—as I have now—find a shady flagstone doorway, and if you don't mind getting a bit of whitewash on your pants, you might—as I am now—put down your backpack and LEAN against it underneath the window of a restaurant where they are playing their Sunday morning tape of a baroque flute concerto grosso instead of the weekday tapes of bouzouki bands.

Sometimes you STAND. This morning I found the tiniest chapel of all so far in Greece, here on the island of Paros, wedged under an overhanging rock next to the sea. Inside the chapel you can see the wink of sea light

Ikaria

in odd places coming in from the one small window, one small door. If you were to be imprisoned here—as surely someone already is—you might grow accustomed to the way the swish of water seems to be responsible for the thick white walls; they are its constant residue. You would notice the spiders, and wonder perhaps idly for a day or two why there were no candles. You might listen for the hoof beats of horses while you were missing light. Two oil-burning votive lamps hang in the perpetual dusk. Is it the soul of a nymph, or a mermaid imprisoned here? I trespass.

As a tourist I have become almost comically aware of the few positional choices available to the human body: sitting, standing, or lying down. And while sitting, standing, or lying down you can remain in one place or move to another one. Quickly or slowly. You can, of course, also spin. (*I woke early, spun in my kitchen with the blue cabinets, whitewashed walls.*)

Steve now confides that he is in love with me, and unless I return his affection, I must stay somewhere else than in his two-roomed house. This is another sudden, unexpected setback. I can't possibly take him seriously (his reputation in this matter would send up all sorts of red flags, even if I were remotely interested). Nonetheless I ruefully admit I ought to work up a bit of sympathy, since in theory at least, he is to me as I am to Mikis. The gods must be giggling somewhere at this bit of triangular foolery they have rigged up for light afternoon amusement. But surely my love for Mikis is deeper, finer, of longer duration than that of my fickle friend! I have cherished it as a deep reeling-into-the-universe-of-who-he-is. Were the ancient Greeks right in regarding love as an illness (Sappho called it "sweet-bitter")? I don't believe that, yet I'm no longer certain about my own definition of love. I book a room in a cheap hotel and take the island bus out to the locally famous "Butterfly Place" for the afternoon.

The bus lets me off at the end of a dirt road leading uphill. In the absence of any signs, buildings, or other people, I start walking up the road. It will lead somewhere, even if not to the Valley of the Butterflies I have been told about.

After a hundred yards or so, a few small whitewashed houses appear on either side of the road. From the black open doorway of one of these, an old woman pops out. She beckons with a skinny arm, "Come!" she says. Suddenly I am precipitated into a dream world again—or rather, the landscape around me takes on a familiar glow that indicates a change in level of reality. The old woman becomes a Crone from every myth and fairy tale on the planet. I shake my head politely and say "Ochi, evharisto" ("No thanks") to her supplication. She is probably hoping to make a few drachmas from me, a tourist, by serving me some kind of food. Stubbornly I plod on up the hill.

The road makes a sharp turn to the right, goes downhill and suddenly I am in a small woods. The road ends at what seems to be a parking lot, and sure enough, I see the word "Petalouthes" ("Butterflies," although in Greek the word means "Flying Flowers"). A few cars are parked, and there is almost total silence. Then I read the many small signs tacked to a row of trees: "Do not Whistle, Do not Clap, Do not Shake the Branches, Do not Wake the Butterflies."

After that I enter the small verdant park, and sure enough, clustered along many twigs and branches I see butterflies with folded wings. I could be in a church full of tiny angels. I almost stop breathing as I gaze and gaze. These butterflies (which are technically some species of moth) come here every year like salmon, to breed and die. They are black and white on the outside, but now and then a butterfly makes a short sleepy flight to a different perch, and a red-orange beam comes stabbing out from the inner lining of the wing—a banked fire.

On and on I wander (tiptoe) into the park, until I realize I have left the compound and gone back to private land again, though there is no outer fence. I come to a stone arch at the end of a narrow path. Beyond it is an iron gate closed and tied with a clothesline. A fig tree stands beside the gate, and beyond it, just through the arch, I can see an overgrown garden. Oleander blooms beneath the huge plane tree in its center, and roses, and I see a single red geranium poking out of the undergrowth. The path continues around to an old villa. It too, is completely overgrown. Nobody has tended this garden in many a long day, but never mind, I recognize it; I was born here, and now for the second time in my life I have been allowed to enter this place. From the other side of the villa, the side away from the garden, I am sure you can glimpse the sea. Likely if I come here again tomorrow, the place will have vanished.

One day in Oregon I began to sing the land. It was a romantic notion I had carried around in my head for fifteen years, from reading Bruce Chatwin's book about Australian Aborigine culture, The Song Lines. *I had no idea what I was doing; it was not so simple as I had first thought it would be.*

I began with the ginko tree in front of my house, which lost all of its leaves in one hour one November afternoon. I opened my mouth and sang, "Ginko tree, which loses all of its leaves in one hour!"

I realized that everything you need to know can be learned this way.

I realized you can't sing the land until you know it; you can't know it until you sing it. I saw two buckets of water set out by the side of the road, and they hit me suddenly as "temporary! temporary!"

You don't have to start with anything. There's no way we will immediately know our land as our ancestors must have done, but we must begin again. I started with the ginko tree, how the leaves fall. Maybe I'll never get any farther than one tree.

I have no reason any more to remain on Paros, yet I still have one week in Greece, so I decide to hop a ferry to Syros, an island I know nothing about. By now I have learned to allow plenty of time for such journeys, since the ferry scheduling system seems to work by logic totally counter to the needs of the passengers. The boats come and go, obviously, you can *see* them. But how on earth does anybody find out when the next boat is leaving? This kind of basic information seems to be guarded by a three-headed dog, one of whose heads is the Port Police who are supposed to be the last word on the subject. The other two heads are the ticketing agencies and people on the street who look like they might know something. Depending on where you want to go, and what kind of boat is usually available to take you there, you may find that it takes an entire day to make the arrangements, during which time you will probably be lied to at least once, and given totally contradictory information several times over, even by the same agency. You might end up having to race back to your room to pack because the friend of a friend has

Ikaria

talked the captain of a day-excursion boat into taking you over to Ikaria if you will just hide your luggage quickly inside before they leave, since he's not supposed to take on any more passengers. Bribes have nothing to do with it; the whole system seems to run like an enormous child's game, the rules of which change constantly and according to whim.

Most of the time, provided you buy the ticket on the same day that you plan to travel, you will be able to walk in and buy a ticket on your first try, and the boat will actually leave within an hour or two of when they tell you it will. To go to Syros, I walked up to the ticket counter an hour before the boat came into port, so had no problem. There seems to be no such thing as the ferry being "full"; they can always crowd one more person aboard.

Sometimes you can climb on early, if you're leaving from Pireaus, for example, the beginning of the ferry's journey. You can snag yourself an inside seat near the window by piling it with all your luggage (which you have just hauled up three flights of stairs), and then go back out to stand at the rail looking down at the dock three stories below. You see cars coming along jammed full of people, luggage strapped to the top; everyone piles out, grandmother takes the baby and the flowered diaper bag while the kids joyfully run their bicycles up the gangplank in front of a couple of motorcycles. All is chaos and total racket.

Out on the sea the ferry is a wonderful power. It throbs beneath you, polluting the sea and air dreadfully. In fact, it is hard to find a breath of fresh air on a ferry, what with upstairs you get the wake of the engine smoke; over the side you get the hot stink of the boat itself; and indoors everybody is smoking and watching terrible American movies with Greek subtitles.

When I came back to Ikaria five years later to go to language school, I took a ferry which arrived in Evdilos after midnight. I stood in the belly of the ferry listening to the screech and rumble as the boat jockeyed for position in front of the jetty. My eyes were on the enormous door, like the bridge of a medieval moat held up by its winches of ropes. The timing of that door's opening is critical: too soon, and the sea will come in. As I watched, the door opened a crack to reveal the whirling stars.

The door went down, more rumble and screech. We surged forward, we scruffy group of passengers, in advance of the trucks and cars and motor bikes. It was 2:30 a.m. in Evdilos, this sweet fishing village I had last seen at 8:30 in the morning almost exactly five years ago to the day. I walked along the sea wall past the group of sleepy people waiting for relatives and friends. I walked past them along the dark waterfront as though I knew exactly where I was going. Maybe because Greek island villages are so small it is possible to learn their shapes and configurations quickly, my feet remembered the land, the stones, the gaps in the wall, the place where it swings away from the sea. All this gave me a heart-filling sense of power, even though I was completely unexpected here, no hotel reservation and the language school not informed of my final choice.

In the dim light from the stars I recognized the particular splay of the buildings around the harbor, the pizza place which was supposed to be turned into a bank, the useless pile of concrete blocks taking up a whole section of harbor over by the shipping office. People clear their throats and look up at the sky when you ask about that. A couple of bars were open. Twenty minutes later I was almost staggering under my backpack as I came up through the garden of a small hotel, rang the night bell and roused the sleepy young man whose father had bought him this hotel when he was 21, six years before. At 3:00 in the morning I stood in my room, looking out at the balcony, the dark bulk of a hill rising on the other side of the road. Hot water in four hours.

Anita Sullivan

Deciding To Go

*That whole morning we were full of joy,
my God, how full of joy.
First, stones leaves and flowers shone
then the sun
a huge sun all thorns and so high in the sky.*
George Seferis

On the eve of my fourth trip to Greece I am in Corvallis sitting at my favorite vegetarian restaurant, alone in the garden in the sun, waiting for lunch to arrive. I have nothing to say. I wonder again how is it possible to maintain a complete self throughout a normal life span? One day's blue is the next day's yellow. I cannot call up at will any interior state of mind and heart from my past, no matter how vivid that state was at the time. I can tell myself the "plot" of an emotionally-charged event: "Oh, yes! That hike up Spencer Butte in the rain on Easter Sunday three years ago with Patrick. He was so very ill. I remember how brown the leaves were on the path, and how cold we both were." I feel the tug of a familiar sadness, but beyond that it is impossible to go. Every segment of life is essentially a secret. Each self passes and cannot be reclaimed.

Why do I believe I want to go to Greece again? This has nothing to do with logic, with ethics, or even with memory. My decision to go again makes no sense. I've already been there three times; I am a single woman in late middle age who has been a financial failure all her life. I haven't the desire to live there permanently, it is not a utopia I seek, or at least not a permanent one. I want to go to Spain and Italy and India and Ethiopia and Brazil and Mongolia and the Orkney Islands: but I want to go to Greece more, much more.

Ikaria

This time I'm returning to Ikaria, even though I've been there before, and probably should broaden my base of exploration. This island is becoming the core of my personal myth about Greece, partly because it is off the beaten path, but truthfully because its name refers to a foolish boy who flew too close to the sun. I identify with that boy. Sure, I know reverting to adolescent behavior as a mature adult is a common experience, but not everyone has the opportunity to live inside the actual landscape of that foolishness, with the chance for what—atonement, re-enactment, a change of heart?

"Ikaria" has been the name of an island in the East-Central Aegean for as long as recorded history; it is spelled "Icaria" equally often. Even though the name is likely pre-Greek in origin, and even if it might have been originally prompted by the island's abundance of fish (old word for "fish"), or its size (a word for "long"), nevertheless very early in history the story of Icarus, his father the wily shaman/engineer Daedalus, and their dramatic escape from the labyrinth in Crete became the favorite source for the island's name. No alternate explanation is ever again needed.

Daedalus and his son Icarus were being held captive in Crete at the palace of King Minos, whose wife Pasiphae had conceived a passion for a bull (one of those bizarre passions that mortals get stuck with when the gods are playing revenge games with each other, as in Shakespeare's *Midsummer Night's Dream*). Daedalus was persuaded against his better judgment to construct a "cow" machine which allowed Pasiphae to seduce the bull, and to everyone's horror and embarrassment she then gave birth to the Minotaur, a sort of bull-human monster who fed on human flesh. Daedalus was then forced to construct a huge labyrinth in the center of the palace grounds so the monster would never escape. As a final insult to his artistry (and likely to insure his silence) he and his son Icarus were imprisoned there.

Daedalus and Icarus built two pairs of enormous wings out of feathers and sticks and glued them to their shoulders with wax. They flew over the walls and headed north towards home. Daedalus cautioned his son not to fly too close to the sun, lest the wax melt, but Icarus was feeling ecstatic at his new freedom and he soon forgot his father's warning. Like many seagoing vessels after him, Icarus was probably defeated by the wild summer *meltemi* winds for which Ikaria is famous (his wax wings having been weakened by the sun), and he plunged to his death in the sea off the coast of an island that ever afterwards, by some strange logic, has been associated with flying. This island is Ikaria.

The irony here is that the island uses an image of a winged Icarus as its chief identifying icon. An abstract double-winged sculpture, monument to Icarus, stands in the harbor at Agios Kirikos, the island's capital. At one time the Greek government was planning to locate an Olympic flying center on the island.

One morning I visited the house of Angelos, an island historian, who lives with his wife, a music teacher, and child in the mountain village of Christos Raches. With characteristic Greek generosity he had set aside time to talk with me about the island's history. I cleared my throat and worked up my courage to speak the obvious truth: "But Icarus *failed!*" He grinned and shrugged. "Icaria," he pointed out, "has long been one of the names for an ideal place." In ancient times it was one of three imaginary lands in the Atlantic, and later, especially in the 18th century, Ikaria became—like Atlantis, Arcadia, and Cythera—part of a small list of literary and artistic icons for "paradise on earth." Karl Marx mentions "Icaria" in his *Manifesto*, apparently referring to Etienne Cabet's mid-nineteenth-century novel *Voyage En Icarie* about an imaginary utopian (and communistic) society. Why did Cabet choose the name Icaria? "Probably all the other good names had already been taken," says Angelos wryly. "Cabet very likely knew nothing of the existence of this island. He was following a literary tradition." Then he added, with a twinkle in his eye, "Maybe if you called your ideal society "Icaria" it meant you were flying from oppression!"

Does this mean we see the tragic death of Icarus, not as just dessert for disobedience, but as an act of faith and longing so strong and beautiful that his actual failure is of no consequence compared to the will and spirit of his attempt? Perhaps Icarus fell into the sea fully satisfied. Still, his father Daedalus flew also, and did *not* fall into the sea, and what island is named after him? I find myself flushed with a specific feeling of exhilarated confusion that I never experience anywhere else but in Greece, and increasingly in Ikaria itself. As if the possibilities for ecstasy and abject misery were suddenly magnified by the peculiar combination of location, topography, accent, slant of sea light, island dialect, gardens, family relationships, bees, springs, boulders, slate, wild herbs that only Ikaria holds.

I have lost my purse in a Cretan hotel. The purse is soft brown leather, a clutch bag; I set it on the counter as I was talking to the receptionist, then walked away for a few minutes to find my two sons, Patrick and Timothy. I am wearing my dark blue raincoat and I am happy. "Μαυρ" I say to the receptionist when I come back, thinking that means "brown" in Greek, but it does not, it means "black." I start searching for it, poking my nose rudely into women's shopping bags as I stroll around the lobby. I have nothing now but the clothes on my back. This has happened before. This has happened before.

    I woke from this dream of Greece. It was Valentine's Day; the alarm was going off in about ten minutes, at 5:25, and I was supposed to get up and start searching the internet for a cheap ticket to Athens. If I'm going over in May, I have to get my ticket early.
    I've already told my friends I'm going back.
    It's a curse, this inability to live with the familiar, the ordinary. I wonder why I have always lunged away from it in a kind of desperation. Last August I bought a ticket for Greece, made reservations to stay in a little room in Nas on Ikaria with a balcony overlooking the sea, then realized I didn't dare to go; I wouldn't have enough for the rent when I got back. So I paid the penalty for forfeiting my ticket, made a few more phone calls to Greece, and felt depressed for several weeks. This year on New Year's Day I had no plans to go anywhere, not *anywhere*, even to visit my sons, or my brother, or my mother, all of whom live in states other than Oregon. About a week ago I changed my mind. The whole process of making arrangements begins again.
    Travel is good practice for dying. You can't really believe you are going away. Yet you have chosen a day to do it, and that day comes. You pack, pick up your bags, walk out and close your door, and put your bags into a car. Now you have taken yourself up from the ground like a weed and you are at the mercy of timelessness again. Who will you be when you return? Where will you go?

    Wanting to travel seems to have little to do with what actually happens on the trip, at least not the gross events. This periodic urge is at least 50% the result of a romantic notion that keeps re-surfacing every time memory fades to a certain weakness. Another Frenchman, Jean-Antoine Watteau painted "The Embarkation for Cythera" between 1704 and 1721. It could as easily have been "The Embarkation for Ikaria," or "for Utopia." A group of travelers waits on the shore with their luggage and picnic baskets, looking across the sea at an island gleaming whitely beneath the clouds. The foreground is in browns and yellows, like reality; the island glimmers in a different dimension, the utopian colors of imagination.

During the times I have traveled to Greece I have had my passport and money stolen, have been sexually assaulted, have gone deeply into debt, have suffered anxiety attacks for weeks in advance, have gone hungry days at a time, have endured chronic indigestion, have been bored, confused, frightened and humiliated. I have also been idiotically happy.

Anita Sullivan

The Gardens

> *At home we have no level runs or meadows,*
> *but highland, goat land. . . .*
> *Grasses, and pasture land, are hard to come by*
> *upon the islands tilted in the sea.*
> *The Odyssey* (Book IV)

Anthropologist Felicitas Goodman outlines five basic ways in which human societies have organized themselves: Hunter-Gatherers, Horticulturalists, Agriculturalists, Nomadic Pastoralists, and City Dwellers. In the chapter on Horticulturalists she says this way of living "disappeared from the scene well over five thousand years ago." She cites a few exceptions. I believe Ikaria is one of them.

There is not enough flat land for agriculture. The island is filled with gardens; people still rely on them as a major source of food year-around. They supplement their vegetables with meat from the goats they raise and hunt, as well as with fish and with any other meat they can find (rabbits, birds). This has been the situation for hundreds, probably thousands of years. Never mind television, cruise ships, video games, internet cafes, automobiles, airports, nude bathing, drugs, and all the other incursions from the later Agricultural and City Dwelling societies. Rhythms of body and mind dictated by the relationship to the natural world can not be easily gainsaid.

In the vegetable garden in the village of Arethousa, Irini tells us they have foxes who sometimes steal their chickens. "They do not steal the children?" someone asks, slightly misunderstanding her Greek, and she laughs and shakes her head. A group of students from the language school is helping her dig up stones, pull weeds, tie up bean plants with scraps of thread. We are spread out along the double terrace high on the side of the mountain in the middle of the island. But we can still see the distant water as a blue mist filling the horizon. On our hands and knees we are joyfully getting dirt under our fingernails, a welcome relief from conjugating verbs. Irini's ten-year-old son seems to have no assigned task, and he splashes barefoot in the irrigation trenches, obviously bored. In Arethousa, says Ifigenia, one of our language school directors, the children go down to the sea alone to swim. Crime is not problem on Ikaria—the police have nothing to do—yet the children do not help in the gardens, they regularly stay up past midnight, and they go down alone to the sea to swim.

My job is to pull weeds in one of the square patches surrounded by a wall of dirt to separate it from other patches full of flourishing vegetables. I have fun tossing stones over the edge of the terrace, hoping they will not bonk some poor rabbit or mouse on the head. This is what Ikarians do every day here.

From the hotel balcony we can see people down on the small valley floor by the sea bent over their rectangular gardens, each patch about 20 feet long and ten feet wide, and divided neatly down the middle the long way by a dirt trench for irrigation. Each garden is subdivided into roughly six small squares, each one outlined by a ridge of dirt, which can be easily breached to let water in. Ikaria is unusual among Greek islands in its abundance of water. It has at least one river in which water runs all year, and many springs, creeks and smaller rivers that drain the central mountain range. The islanders have taken full advantage of this resource, and organized a (seemingly) efficient system to distribute water by collecting it in strategically-located black plastic cisterns, to each of which is connected a row of narrow black hoses. Each hose is regulated by a faucet, and people take turns as to which day their personal faucet is "on." In a sense, the hoses have almost taken the place of the streams: there is no terrace so remote, no hillside so steep or rocky, that doesn't have at least one hose crossing it or running alongside it, and you can hear the sound of gurgling and rushing water through these narrow, man-made "streams" wherever you go. I would imagine that repairing leaks in the island hose system might be the equivalent of keeping the fences fixed in the Old West.

    The gardens look like raised beds, but actually the dirt walls that surround each patch are the highest thing in the garden, making the growing spaces slightly sunken hollows. Many of the gardens are walled by piles of stones, usually about two or three feet high. Some garden patches are fallow, filled with weeds, and goats are often tethered inside on a stake to graze down the grass—sometimes cows. A path always runs between the gardens, and seems to be open for anyone to walk through. Nobody hollers, "This is private property, keep out" as we traipse through with our bathing suits to the beach. People look up and smile and say hello.

    All over Ikaria, up and down the steep hillsides, are terraces held in place by stone retaining walls. Most of the terraces are now overgrown by grass, with a few stumps of old grape vines, giving a sweet sense of civilized wilderness. The land has been tilled for thousands of years, as is typical in this part of the world. Yet nowadays most of the gardens are in the lowlands, the relatively few flat areas where the sea takes a dip inland to make a small beach. Apparently the terraces were used in ancient times for wine grapes, and more recently to grow grain and olives. It is more difficult to farm up on the hillsides, and until and unless Ikaria becomes once again a wine-exporting island, the small permanent population of 8,000 to 9,000 can fulfill its needs more easily on lower ground.

One afternoon my friend Pamela from Oregon took me up to the tiny village of Kato Proespera (a "suburb" of the larger village of Proespera). It was quite hot on the dirt road, and she wanted to find the spring she remembered was "around here somewhere." We turned off the road into the yard of a little church, and found a path leading down into a likely looking patch of bushes. As we came down the path we met an old man carrying two buckets, and after a short conversation it turned out he was heading for the same spring, and would take us there.

We sat in the shade beside the small muddy pool while the old man waded in with his black rubber boots and began to pull stones and old rags out of a hole in the bottom, so the water that had collected behind the rock and concrete wall would run out into the irrigation ditches to his little farm nearby. This is the old system, before the plastic cisterns and hoses came into place. A community would dam up a small creek and use one of the flat slabs of island slate for a ready-made gate. Rather than regularly pulling up the gate, they would dig a drain hole at the bottom, and then take turns as to which day they are allowed to let the water loose into the ditches. Like many of the Ikarians in the villages, this old man looked to be in his 70's, and was doing all the farm work himself; his children were in Athens, his wife up on the mountain in the larger village of Christos Raches, at their winter house.

I decided to wade into the water myself for a quick dip, but as I was edging my way across a muddy boulder near the spring at the head of the pool, I slipped suddenly and banged my cheek hard on the rock, almost knocking myself unconscious. The old man became quite agitated, but when I kept saying "eimai kala" ("I'm fine"), he finished his work. After he was done, he signaled that we should follow him to his little house, where he would administer some kind of treatment. Pamela and I sat in the yard on a couple of old broken down chairs while he went inside and rummaged around, finally reappearing with a wad of newspaper and a plastic bottle of olive oil. He doused the newspaper with oil and rubbed my bruised cheek, referring to himself with a little grin as "O yiatros," the doctor. Then he brought us an enormous bowl of apricots from his orchard, and we sat awhile together in the sun. All around us were the fruits of his labors: apple trees, grape vines, olive trees, and a vegetable garden. Bees were loud in the blossoms. It seems the Ikarians have arranged their growing so that the season is long, something is ripe from May through September, and yet things are in bloom also during that time.

I felt bad for having become a nuisance to the old man, and possibly interrupting his work, but he seemed not to mind. We set off with a huge plastic bag of apricots. My cheek did not swell at all, as it well should have with such a blow. It was only mildly bruised for a few days.

Across from the student hotel in Evdilos the little man in the dark blue trousers waters his garden every morning. A pocket-sized garden: fistful of lettuce, cucumber vine, row of tomatoes, one small cherry tree. I can see the top of his bald head as he stands patiently holding the curved hose, which he has just connected to a community faucet some 25 yards away, the hose stretching across the concrete floor of a construction site. I am certain he is very ordinary.

Why do the scales not fall from my eyes? A deep continuous humming of bees is not drowned out by the English sparrows, the motor bikes, the clunk and rattle of construction. Whenever I come back to Greece a whole section of my brain is blocked out, and another one activated instead. Today, for example, I simply could not call to mind the word "tamari." I saw a cat cross a village street and suddenly I remembered Oregon rain. Every moment here is like that—small openings into former silver caves. Nouns become things that appear, rise, spread, glow, flap in front of my eyes, and in back of me a rhythm rolls out. The chorus hums. Words dissolve in the sun every minute and re-form like clouds, totally undisciplined. My eyes see a sudden cluster of flowers, a butterfly, an emaciated cat in a doorway, a dirty village path in front of my feet through weeds, a garden, and each of these things is equally able to stir my heart to a small frenzy. This is not the normal hierarchy at work. Surely the world cannot remain in such a highly-charged state for the island's inhabitants as it does for me; here only, not back at home in Oregon. How did this come to be? Was it because I came here originally, five years ago, in such a state of high passion, and gradually I have exchanged one passion for another? That makes for good theory, and there might have been truth in it during those first painful two months I spent in this country. But Ikaria truly is extraordinary; even some of the local people call it paradise.

I feel myself growing accustomed to this place, deeper and deeper every day as if traveling back along a simple path through the manifold layers of my own individual origin. Perhaps in the long run, having followed that path as far as I have been able to in these years of visiting Greece will compensate for the great failures in my life, which I still fear. I had a memory of Mikis today, with that dark, cautious way he used to have of looking across the table at me, as if I truly were ill and might burst forth volubly and irrationally at any moment. I thought how useless it was that I expended so much energy trying to clear a path between us. He had no idea how pure I am. And I had no idea what in him is of equal quality and magnitude to this purity. Eventually, to keep from doing him damage, I became silent. We entirely missed one another, I believe, through equal and opposite purity.

Ikaria

Having a Coffee

*If I can't drink my bowl of coffee
three times daily
then in my torment I will shrivel up
like a piece of roast goat.*
        J.S. Bach, *The Coffee Cantata*

Coffee in the morning before 9:00 is not always readily at hand in a Greek village. Therefore, when I wake up I'm like a small animal engaged in the daily struggle for survival. A furless creature, I stumble across the veldt, sniffing the air, watching for signs of fellow humans, and prepared to execute invasive feints followed by pleading or even demanding gestures.

After completing two weeks at the language school, I'm staying in the village of Nas, three miles up the road from Armenistis. I found this place through my friend Pamela, who has taken over from her husband in leading the small tour group that first introduced me to this island. Gradually I'm building my own network of acquaintances on Ikaria: learning who disapproves of whose lifestyle, which people it is safe to mention in the company of so-and-so, and most importantly, who is related to whom.

The first morning I come down the stairs and find the door of the restaurant locked. Thea and Eleas are not to be blamed for sleeping in, since their last customer may not have left till long after midnight. So, I start down the packed dirt road to check out the other three tavernas in this tiny village. Sure enough, the kitchen door is open in one of the rival restaurants, the one that sprawls along the top of the cliff overlooking the best beach on the island. I poke my head inside. "Boro na echo ena kafe, parakalo?" I ask in my sweetest voice. In Greece you don't ask for "coffee" but for "a coffee," an endearing distinction. The lady in the dark print dress is standing immobilized by a kitchen full of dirty dishes from the night before. She promises to bring me one, and I go out to find a spot near the wall, away from the early morning breeze.

    At a nearby table a man sits and smokes, gazing across the vine-shaded terrace to the sea. He already has his little cup of Greek coffee. I have ordered the alternative, Nescafe, out of sheer pity, figuring it would be easier to make. We don't speak. Three days later I make his acquaintance and find out he is an electrician from Athens who comes here every year for holiday. I have become slightly paranoid about Greek men. They seem indifferent to my age in a cheerful and foraging spirit of "we take what we can get." There is scarcely such thing as conversation between female tourists and single Greek men just for the sake of passing the time of day, unless you firmly stay put at your own table and make sure you mention you are married (which I am not, but never mind). Ironically, Mikis had zero interest in me back in Oregon, and that's partly because there were plenty of available females his age. I sip my mediocre coffee and muse about this. What would I have done if, in the coffee shop he had acted like so many of the men do over here, asking you out for "a coffee" and then, settling into a dark corner and almost immediately sliding a hand up the inside of your shirt while poking his tongue into your ear? Never mind that you couldn't pull something like that off in a public coffee shop in Oregon, this kind of predatory behavior hardly even qualifies as sexual, and is carried out with a lack of aggression, even a casual boredom that could be amusing if it weren't so distasteful.

    What response from Mikis did I actually desire? I would get weak in the knees when I saw him across the room, my heart would pound, and I could feel my veins fill with a hot liquor of longing. But when I tried to imagine going off to bed with him—pretending we were the same age—even back then before my first trip to Greece, my brow would start to furrow. Yes, I got out in the nick of time. That last night would have put me over the edge of madness if I had given up the trip and stayed behind like some tragic heroine committing an act of courage she knows will carry the death penalty. Coming to Greece, strangely enough, propelled by that negative emotional energy poised to destroy me, and the constant ducking away from it like a pursued maiden who turns herself into a laurel tree . . . . Coming to Greece has had the opposite effect of a nervous breakdown; from the beginning I have been almost manic in my attitude to the place. And this mania has not worn off. It has not worn off.

Yiannis showed me how to make Greek coffee in the tiny kitchen of their "snack shop and bar." Almost every time I stop in at Charlie's place, whether I'm staying in the room upstairs or not, they offer me a coffee and won't let me pay. In fact if you have coffee with a Greek, the only way you can ever pay for it is to excuse yourself to go inside to the bathroom and stop off at the counter on the way in. Sometimes you can't even get away with that if your timing is not quick enough. It's part of the huge network of relationships—family and friends, family and strangers, strangers as guests—that underlies the whole culture. Everybody knows everybody else and is in constant touch, either directly or by phone. The cell phone culture of constant communication already existed in Greece for centuries.

One afternoon when two friends and I were renting an apartment for a week on Patmos we invited the landlord's mother over for a coffee. "Five o'clock Sunday afternoon," we cajoled her sweetly in our best student Greek. We had no idea if she would actually come when we issued our invitation just after she had stopped by with an apron-full of fresh tomatoes from her garden. But Kyria Katerina arrived promptly at 5:00, beaming, with her daughter Fotini who lives next door. We served Nescafe, watermelon and baklava in our rented kitchen and talked about life on Patmos, about the water shortage and the changes that the old woman has observed on the island during her life here. Fotini's daughter had just graduated from high school and that very afternoon was giving a party for her friends in celebration. "Everybody used to live eight or ten people inside one small house," Kyria Katerina said with a wide smile. "Now each child has his or her own room. Everybody has so much now, and they are not happy." Judging by the way Fotini also smiled, we realized we had tapped into a vein of family aphorism. But coming from this large, warmhearted woman, mother of five and grandmother to something like twenty, the words sounded truly wise.

In Greece, drinking coffee is a ritual that loosens the tongue as much as wine does, but perhaps in a different way. Once in a hotel in Athens I entered the morning coffee room for my complimentary breakfast, and sat down in an easy chair next to a stranger, a much younger man. We had barely exchanged polite greetings when the maid appeared with trays and set them down in front of us on the table, giving us a common sugar bowl and butter dish as if we were a married couple. We looked at each other in some amusement and the maid put her hands up to her face with a little cry. "I didn't know," she said in Greek. "No problem," the young man and I both replied at the same time, to alleviate her distress. She kept trying to change us back to complete strangers again, but it was too late. Morning coffee for foreigners like us operates in a neutral zone; it implies no hidden agenda, no future obligations. We could handle it.

Anita Sullivan

Wilderness

Like a bird with a broken wing
who has been traveling for years
through the air
like a bird who can no more
endure the air and its storms,
so evening falls.
    George Seferis

"Sparrow" could be a Greek verb. If so, it would be rangy and restless but small in scope. It would have to mean something other than "hope," as a similar verb "spero" does in Latin; maybe, like the bird, it could describe some ordinary but useful task done every day, as opposed to the flashy fuss and bother which just wears things out. Probably "sparrow" would be an intransitive verb, preferring to insulate itself from direct responsibility with a protective sprinkle of prepositions; yet active rather than passive in voice, and—like the bird—of an ancient but borrowed lineage, having been tucked in at the last minute by Odysseus as carefully as an egg, into a soft and secret corner of his whimsical backpack as he set out at long last for Ithaca.

  One day a group of us walked across the entire island. Along the way we saw no wild animals, not even any of the island's famous brown snakes, but we did see some birds, including a wild falcon.
  "This will be a hike of two, maybe three hours," Mihalis (the language school's other director) told us a few days before, when the students were inquiring about our "local culture" plan for the weekend. We would pick up an old footpath, he said, somewhere on the mountainside above Evdilos, and walk directly over the mountain to Agios Kirikos in time for lunch. People

used to do this all the time before automobiles arrived in the late sixties.

"Like this, Mihali?" Carol spread out her arms and pretended to be inching her way across a narrow cliff face, looking nervously down into the abyss below. Mihalis shook his head vigorously. "No, nothing like that. This is not a dangerous walk, we know these paths. We will have a guide."

At 8:00 Saturday morning we stopped to pick up Costas, our guide. His mother tried to hand him the black and tan goatskin water bag, but he refused to take it. He climbed into the car with us carrying only a pack of cigarettes. We all had our backpacks full of water, fruit, crackers, sunscreen, extra socks, maps, cameras. Soon we parked on a wide place in one of the switchbacks, piled out of the car and started up a narrow dirt strip, which looked to me just like another goat path.

"How do you tell a goat path from a foot path?" I asked Mihalis. He insisted that the "monopatia," the human footpaths, had all been painstakingly constructed years ago with rock retaining walls to support many flat paving stones set down along the steep slopes. And the fact that the goats used the human paths too did not mean they were goat paths. And the fact that these monopatia extended for miles, so that large sections of them were just strips of packed dirt between the bushes (no more paving stones), did not make them goat paths. Many times I would see a "path" meandering off between the rocks, and wonder why Costas had ignored it. Maybe he had a sixth sense. Or maybe, like the Australian Bushmen, he had sung the land so long he knew each piece of it by name.

The Ikarians have now mapped many of these trails, aided by a team of young volunteers from the

European Economic Community. Previously everybody knew where they were, and maps were not needed. The paths were maintained by the islanders in a somewhat organized way; their goats browsed the vegetation to keep the weeds from overgrowing the flat stones, and frequent traffic also kept the vegetation at bay.

But today, apparently, we were deliberately deviating from the main route across the mountain, and instead following a shorter, alternate system of paths suggested to Costas by the bus driver. "Take the shortcut" he must have told Costas, as they nodded together and agreed, "Yes, these tourists are soft, they probably can't handle the usual path that we take every week when we go over to Agios Kirikos to hunt birds." Bird hunting is an old sport in Greece, unfortunately often involving the shooting of small migratory birds simply for fun because they make easy targets.

So, we took the shortcut. In about two hours we began to lose our way on a regular basis. Sometimes we were crawling under thickets that we didn't have the strength to push out of the way because the branches were so stiff and wiry. We scrambled over boulders across rushing streams, and we pulled ourselves up the steep sides of slopes with rocks slipping rapidly out from under our feet. Carol's dramatic mime had become a reality. We were, indeed, on the edge of a precipitous cliff inching our way along, while far below we could see a small river emptying into the sea. The silence was broken only by distant goat bells and the sound of erratic avalanches of small pebbles.

We came once into a valley forested by small, dark, twisted trees. Above us floated a peregrine falcon, its queer face split by brown stripes. We gaped at him through Mihalis' binoculars, knowing we were witnessing a rare event. At the top of the final mountain peak, after six hours of hiking, Costas smoked a cigarette while we finished the last of our water. Our spirits were good. Only two more hours and we would be in Agios Kirikos.

At other times on the island I saw snakes; there were owls visible in the daytime landing on the roof beside the school; we knew there were foxes around. But on this hike we saw none of these creatures. The riskiest part of the trip was the drive back over the mountain with Costas at the wheel.

I dreamed that I was driving slowly down a wide city street, early in the morning. There was no traffic except for a woman on a skateboard riding down the middle of the street. I looked back as I went past and saw that she was pushing a blue sofa in front of her, also on wheels. Her hair was blowing and she looked happy. "She must be moving her furniture this way," I thought in admiration. "What a neat way to move!"

Sitting on the porch of the Snack Bar with Yiannis one morning I asked him, a young single guy in his middle twenties, if he ever got tired of living on Ikaria and wanted to leave. In his usual quiet, thoughtful way he smiled and shook his head. "If I didn't have the mountains, I would have been gone from here long ago," he said. "I go up into the mountains with my gun to hunt." He looked at me and stopped. "I know you probably don't approve of hunting." I nodded ruefully, not telling him I was pretty close to being an animal rights activist. He probably had that figured out anyway. "I shoot rabbits for eating. Sometimes I just walk around. I like the *idea* that I can get lost up there." He waved his hand at the Atheras mountain range, which runs lengthways along the middle of the island.

Unlike many other Greek islands, Ikaria actually has some wilderness. Or rather, there is a hierarchy of abandonment here on Ikaria as in the entire Mediterranean basin, rather than the clear distinction between wilderness and ordinary outdoors that we have set up in the United States. Every time I fly east from Portland, Oregon, I am amazed to look down at vast stretches of desert, forest and mountain with no buildings in sight. We are brought up to believe nobody has *ever* lived in these remote regions, and though very likely untrue, this belief infuses a mixture of fear, mystery and relief into our collective image of our nation. But here on Ikaria you always know, no matter which rock or patch of ground you set your shoe down upon, somebody else's foot has been there, more than once, before you. During the past eight or nine thousand years, entire villages may have sunk into the ground beneath your feet. This knowledge alters the quality of the silence up in the hills. It causes you to sniff the air, to move, to hold your head as if you were expecting something.

"Are there any wild animals left here?" I asked.

"No," he said sadly. "Even the deer were hunted out a long time ago. On the mainland there are wild boar, even some lions. But not here."

On Ikaria the hunters still pick up their guns and head for the mountains. Maybe they don't really care any more if they actually kill anything. Maybe they would be just as happy with binoculars, if the tradition came to allow it. Maybe they will have to start hunting English sparrows soon.

The English sparrows make a deafening roar from the eaves of a deserted house across the alley from the hotel. "Cheep! Cheep!" is all they have to say, in resonating numbers. They live between the rocks where the plaster is falling out. The windows are boarded up, in turquoise. These birds have taken over the islands now, at least in the villages. The Mediterranean tradition of shooting migratory birds apparently ignores them, thus they have moved in to fill an ecological gap. They are urban birds, incredibly versatile in their eating habits, resistant to the commotion and pollution of humans in much the same way pigeons are. If only the starving cats could be trained to hunt sparrows, some sort of natural balance might be regained. I weep for the birds that have been replaced, but who ever knows these things?

Anita Sullivan

The Naming of Things

I'd found a good name to fill up with someone.
from a Swampy Cree Indian poem

What is it about certain small events that makes you notice them sometimes, as if skeletons were actually made of mosaic, not of the cells of bone?

I wanted to mail some books home so I wouldn't have to carry them in my luggage. This happens a lot to tourists. We try to bring books we can read and discard, on shelves in hotels or in people's homes—but then somebody gives us a replacement or two. Or maybe we've bought a couple of rugs and some bottles of honey, which weigh as much as one entire suitcase full of clothes. The thought of lugging that extra weight up the ferryboat stairs or through the narrow streets of the Plaka in Athens is intolerable. So, near the end of my second stay on Ikaria, I found myself at the Evdilos post office, expecting a lengthy and expensive ordeal.

In preparation, I had scrounged a box from a grocery store, leaving it open so the postal officials could look inside if they chose, and I had bought a roll of packing tape to close it up again. Lacking scissors, I brought my all-purpose kitchen knife, the one with the bright pink handle, to cut the tape.

At the takidromeo they laughed when they saw my box and my tape and my knife. The tall thin postman looked at me, squinting slightly. "I saw you at the panigiri last night, yes?" he smiled. I had been up in a mountain village the previous evening with a group of students from the school, for a festival. The postman had danced with Sophia, a classmate, most of the evening. He was a manic dancer, and Mihalis told us he has been battling some chronic illness such as multiple sclerosis (the translation in Greek was a bit sketchy), and that he has heart trouble as well. Already I know small things about people on the island after living here for a month. Local people wave to me from their motor bikes, from behind counters in stores and restaurants, on beaches.

The dancing postman looked carefully down the list of countries to find the rate for a package to the U.S. After awhile he frowned and picked up the phone. Apparently the United States of America was not on the list. While I waited, he and the younger more burly postman served other customers around me. My postman consulted his colleague, who flipped the page back and ran his finger down the long sheet of paper until he came to "Etats Unis." Since French used to be the chief second language in Greece, the U.S. is still listed this way in their reference book.

When they weighed my box they both looked concerned and burst into a heated discussion. I understood, with my limited Greek, that the box needed to be broken into two smaller packages to make it cheaper to send. But they wouldn't hear of me taking it back. They pulled out a couple of padded envelopes from an old file cabinet and I stood at the counter and re-packed all my goods inside. When I walked out of the post office forty five minutes late for class, I felt like a princess.

This morning on the hotel veranda eating breakfast, I thought I heard someone whisper my name. It was very clear, in the old familiar way that Mikis used to pronounce it, with the "T" sounding crisp and clear, not soft like a "D." I realized how primal that is. You are touched into life by the sound of your name directed towards you by someone who already knows you. I imagined myself traveling alone around the world trying to recover from an old sorrow, and suddenly after years of being in different nameless hotels listening to the babble of voices in various tongues, I heard someone call my name.

Every time I come to Ikaria I end up going to Theoktistis, one of the more accessible monasteries. It is a regular Saturday or Sunday afternoon outing for the students. "Theoktistis" means "built by god," and the name refers to a way of constructing houses, or churches, out of native island stone. Ikaria has enormous boulders, many of which have configured themselves conveniently so that they could be a roof or a wall for a house. Just stuff a few extra stones in between the overhanging rock and the ground, and you have your dwelling place. This monastery includes a small "Theoktistis" chapel up on a remote hillside, with a huge stone roof which makes the little church underneath look as if it is being squashed by some giant's careless shoe. The fairy-tale effect is enhanced by the tiny red door at the top of a short set of ladder-like stairs.

"St. Theoktistis," Mihalis tells us on our first visit, with an entirely straight face, "is buried somewhere else, but this monastery was named after her." He sweeps his hand around to include the little white church with the Byzantine paintings, the small outbuildings, and further up the hill the tiny chapel. I am puzzled. How could there be a real person named after a geological process? I remember what Gilbert Murray said about the origin of the gods: *When the initiated young men of Crete or elsewhere danced at night over the mountains in the Oreibasia or Mountain Walk they not only did things that seemed beyond their ordinary workaday strength; they also felt themselves led on and on by some power which guided and*

Ikaria

sustained them. This daemon has no necessary name: a man may be called after him 'Oreibasius,' 'Belonging to the Mountain Dancer,' just as others may be named 'Apollonious' or 'Dionysius'.

Later I realize my mistake when I learn of the Byzantine St. Theoktiste of Lesbos, whose bones are now reputed to be resting comfortably "somewhere else" on this very island. The Ikarians have happily appropriated this saint, and conflated her with their own collective spirit, to carry for them the power that comes out of the mysterious huge stones with which their countryside is so graced. Paros, Syros, Patmos, Samos—these other islands I have visited do not have such stones, nor a buried saint by that name either.

Inside the tiny chapel with the enormous roof we almost trip over a trunk full of bones. It's protruding from a niche near the front entrance, like a square peg that tried to fit into a round hole. The trunk is not locked, and when we raise the lid like adventurous children, we find inside a small collection of old skulls. Carefully we lift them out, these yellowed bones. We are unaccustomed to handling human skulls, and we wonder aloud if these might have been the monks alive here 300 years ago; we yearn for their names, their stories. There are no signs saying "show respect for the bones," or "please don't touch." Gently, we replace them. I can't help but wonder if this trunk serves as a kind of toy box for children on church days, but that is probably a sinful thought.

Sometimes the need for a name comes first—as in the case of "St. Theoktistis"; but sometimes a name just appears in the air as a sound, and begs to be filled up with its own person. I had promised Yiannis that I would not leave Ikaria without finding a name for the kitten who lived on their front porch. But I didn't want to just make something up. Besides, I had truly forgotten my casual promise by the time several weeks had passed. Then one day a group of us were bumping along a back road in a jeep, somewhere between Nas and Karkinagri. We passed a lovely orchard of citrus trees, and the owner came out to chat with us. We were admiring his oranges and lemons, but the driver, who was probably Pericles, pointed to a tree that didn't look quite like all the others, and had a smaller fruit. "What's that one?" he asked. "Mousmouliá," the man said with a note of pride in his voice. In the back seat I leafed madly through my dictionary. "Loquat" was the closest equivalent, though I don't believe it is exactly right. But I sat in a happy daze all the way through the rest of the trip, repeating the word at irregular intervals so I wouldn't forget it. "Mousmouliá," a perfect name for the small kitten. When I told Yiannis he threw back his head with a thoughtful look and rolled the word around on his tongue. Then he grinned. I have no idea what happened after that.

Ikaria

Moni Mounte

> *I am contented, for I know that Quiet wanders laughing*
> *and eating her wild heart among pigeons and bees....*
>   William Butler Yeats

The first time I walked up the mountain from Armenistis to Christos Raches I felt as if I had disappeared into a different time. As I came around the last switchback to the outskirts of the village, I passed a small sign pointing off down an even narrower dirt road, "Moni Mounte" it said mysteriously.

Leafing through my chunky little dictionary I found that "moni" means "monastery," but it's an old word for it, not much in common use any more. In English there really is no such thing as two words meaning exactly the same thing: each time a word tries to do that, it immediately gets overgrown with mosses and barnacles of nuances, until it ceases to resemble its original self. In Greek this doesn't seem to happen; words just go off into the bushes and crouch down to wait for somebody to remember them.

On my first hike up this mountain I kept on going towards town. Instead of a monastery I went into a gas station and spent a long morning visiting with Nama, who is Koula and Charlie's niece. She and her husband and baby girl live in a tiny spotless apartment behind the gas station, where she spends her days washing innumerable loads of laundry and hanging them out to dry on the roof. I sat in the kitchen drinking homemade retsina out of a coke bottle and gossiping about babies with the landlady and various cousins who dropped by.

Although you can catch glimpses of the sea from Raches, and from most of the other mountain villages on Ikaria, the seven or eight or ten miles that distances

Anita Sullivan

these villages from the coast signals an entire change of philosophy. Yiorgos explained this to me one day when a group of us were strolling around Evdilos after dinner. He was born in Raches and although he now lives and works in Evdilos right by the water, he says his character was formed in the mountains. "Coast people are soft," he grinned, and the comparison went on from there as he quickly sketched for me some of the subtleties resulting from this duality, by which a person's character is shaped either through the backbone of the land or the open fluidity of the sea: open and closed, hard and soft, and from there into humor, how you discipline your children, even how you dance (with severe vigor and precision, or more wildly, less accurately). This is an ancient duality around the Mediterranean, well documented by travel writers, and it was neat to hear it from a kind of original source.

"Me," I told him with a grin, "I'm just a tourist on a rope swing in the garden at Moni Mounte, where I have a glorious view of the sea."

He shook his head, admonishing me. "But up there the sea is far away, far away."

In Oregon I discovered that my friend Pamela had also swung on the same tree swing at Moni Mounte. Sitting over our coffee we laughed with amazement when we realized we were able to describe precisely an area the size of our sitting-bones in a country nine time zones away. Talking with her of the monastery, I had another big understanding about myself and Mikis. He is a seacoast person; I am a mountain person. Such a distinction goes quite deep.

"I am contented, for I know that Quiet wanders laughing and eating her wild heart among pigeons and bees," said Yeats in, "In the Seven Woods," and I decided at age 12 this was what I wanted engraved on my cemetery headstone.

"Probably just as well Mikis and I never got together." I was able to poke fun at myself now, years later, without bitterness. "Like Romeo and Juliet: the marriage would never have lasted," I added, taking an idea to its logical absurdity. Is that what mountain people do in their hours of silence among the stones?

Moni Mounte is a monastery on Ikaria that used to house a small group of nuns, not monks, another surprise. On the postcard for sale up in the village, the white church tower is almost dead center, leaning slightly forward as if pulling the church out from behind its screen of dark cypress trees. It could be a magnificent finger pointing out of the wilderness, proclaiming some metaphorical truth about the persistence of religion (if it could be *here*, it could be anywhere). Except that in Greece, it is in remote spots like this where a church is *most* likely to be found. Stories exist about the name: "Mounté" means "Count" in Italian, and the monastery was supposedly built by an Italian Count, maybe in the 13th century. All very logical, except that nobody has any idea who this Italian nobleman was, and a dark intimation lurks behind the smiles of Ikarians that the real name of the place is something else entirely—as with St. Theoktistis, or Ikaria itself—a name that everybody knows except us tourists who rely upon road signs to tell us where we are. In winter, amid the traditional mountain fogs, Moni Mounte might disappear altogether, randomly, for weeks on end.

In high summer tourists are invited to support the upkeep of the buildings by purchasing post cards and soft drinks in what might have once been the community's refectory. There is enough within its gated walls to occupy a busload for a maximum of half an hour, if the church is unlocked. Besides church and refectory, the walls enclose a couple of houses for nuns (no longer in residence), an outbuilding or two, and a wide paved courtyard. Below the monastery the slopes are covered with a tangle of olive and apple trees, dipping gradually into a valley forested with pines and scrub oak which, centuries ago, may have been carefully held at bay.

Two modest graves lie just below the wall behind the church. They are almost identical in material (marble) and design, but almost 100 years apart. The first says "Theoktisti, 1878," and the second "Irini, 1991." Irini, the last nun to reside here, was in her 80's when she died. Could the first grave be that of St. Theoktistis, whom Mihalis referred to as having been buried "somewhere else"? No, of course that's impossible, the date is a thousand years too late.

I imagine Pamela on the old rope swing at Moni Mounte. In my image she is wearing a yellow dress for some reason—maybe that's how I would like to look myself whenever I am there. Then I see the actual swing, a photograph someone took of me in my old yellow shorts climbing happily onto the wobbly board between long ropes. The scene could be a photo or a painting. In the valley below, the silver of the olives is punctuated occasionally by the severe, finger-like cedars. Here I begin to believe in the Doctrine of Signatures—the Renaissance philosophy of natural magic by which connections are made between objects in the natural world by means of a system of outward signs—the sun shines onto the tops of the oak leaves, darkness on their undersides, so they are set up to make clear but infinitely varying shadows. Thus are we invited to make our own distinctions.

When I am at Moni Mounte I can feel the tentative energy of the forest covering this meager earth. These would not be the original trees of ancient times, excepting perhaps, the olives. For centuries the Ikarians made a living by exporting charcoal, which they burned out of their abundant trees. For centuries there were more trees than Ikarians, and this remained a sustainable enterprise. Then about 150 years ago, the trees were overtaken at last. The island was no longer lush, but came to deserve the adjective "bare," just like most other Greek islands. You can see rubble, tree stumps, sand, thorny shrubs; you can see the rocks (βράχοι), or are they stones (πέτρες)? Recent forest fires have further reduced the number of trees and left new versions of bare landscape. Browsing goats run loose all over the island and further discourage new trees from reaching maturity. Who knows how quickly the forests might return if goats were kept confined? Sometimes if I listen carefully I can hear the garble the old olive trees use for code among themselves between sleeps.

Nevertheless, the view from Moni Mounte is of trees and sea, green and blue. Many, many greens and many, many blues. Earth, air, fire, and water have shifted together here in ways that are timeless. Who are we, mostly water, to think we can substantially interfere for long?

Rocks have been plundered too. Somewhere in the middle of the nineteenth century the poor residents of Christos Raches finally gave in to temptation and raided the 6th century B.C. temple of Artemis at Nas for stones to build a church they called "Christos Metamorphosis." A long process of metamorphosis was finally complete, one temple declining into another.

Anita Sullivan

Artemis' small "nas" (chapel) had lasted for centuries on a hill by the sea at the mouth of the Chalares River. Today little is visible to indicate whatever might be the temple's history; serious excavation has never taken place. The tumbled rocks around the remains of the building's floor are scarcely distinguishable from their wild brethren dotting the steep hillside above.

Two women swing at Moni Mounte, with no knowledge of the earlier group of women who lived here, their daily rituals. On the single stone house, whitewashed only on the front face, dark shuttered windows gently close off the interior. We don't know who to ask for the key to the church. Has the church spawned its tiny chapel, hidden further up the hill beneath an overhanging boulder, to allow local access to the chthonic powers of this place? Who painted the red iron gate with the yellow cross? Red and yellow, colors of the Archangel Michael, the lord of fire and sun. White walls, red gate: red and white, colors of cinnabar, container of the Primary Fluid, the Stone that is not always a stone.

The Ikarians consistently retreated to the hills to avoid the ravages of pirates, or Turks, or Slavs, or Arabs. The history of the island can be summed into a tale of survival by appearing and disappearing; going to the mountains, coming back down to the sea. People constructed small stone houses without chimneys, and lived in poverty and discomfort the likes of which are hard to imagine, sometimes slowly choking to death in the smoke which they dared not let rise above the trees. Fire and earth. Surely their long years of silence and endurance must have sent into the air a vigorous folkloric energy, filled with thousands of lost stories.

The stone wall around the monastery is a link between earth and sky. Its stones are very old, held in

Ikaria

place by their own hardened dust, a natural lime. Sitting there on the wall's broad and whitewashed surface, I can feel cold seeping up, and because I am slightly drunk with the air of the place, I imagine this cold to be primal—Earth's own self stirring, a fractal infinity roiling inside an outward sprinkling of stones. What are we doing when we move these stones around, when we arrange them into walls or houses?

  Sitting on the swing at Moni Mounte, I can see the Mediterranean as a blue mist, and mostly would not guess it was water at all unless I knew this ahead of time. The sea is a different sea when your body is out of its range.

Anita Sullivan

Bathing

*I have desired to go
Where springs not fail
To fields where flies no sharp and sided hail
And a few lilies blow.*

*And I have asked to be
Where no storms come,
Where the green swell is in the havens dumb,
And out of the swing of the sea.*
                            Gerard Manley Hopkins

Some people actually swim in the ocean, and I'm not one of them. When I lived for a spell of weeks on the island of Grand Cayman in the Caribbean, I was surprised to discover that many of the native peoples there did not know how to swim. Possibly they see the ocean and its immediate shoreline as more important for other things, such as food and travel. Many beach-loving tourists don't swim either, they merely "take dips" between long spells of lying on the sand.

To my mind, the most important function of a good beach is to provide a place to walk barefoot on a level surface, preferably for miles. Oregon beaches are exactly right for walking this way, since the coastline is public, and the weather is almost invariably too cold for swimming. All year long, but especially in winter, it's the custom to put on your windbreaker, roll up your jeans, carry your shoes and socks in your backpack, and then decide if you'll stride into the wind first or on the way back. After an hour or so, your mind is clear and you are justified in stopping by a café for a coffee or a glass of wine. People swim and surf in the northwest ocean, but they most certainly do not bathe there.

In the Mediterranean you can bathe. You can float around in the quiet water like a jellyfish, or dive around like a mermaid, or bask like a princess in her private pool. Not every day, of course: this is a real ocean much of the time, with whitecaps foaming and raging at the rocks, and shipping traffic brought to a standstill. Nevertheless, on the days when the sea is behaving like a lake, as Yiannis calls it, you can understand fully why "edge of glass" is one of the Greek words for seashore.

My schoolmates from Luxembourg and Germany come to Greece as their best outlet to the sea. They love to swim and to lie for hours on the sand reading. Since I like neither to swim much, nor to lie around in the sand, I learned to appreciate Greek beaches for a variety of different reasons. The tiny whitewashed houses that are built right up to the edge of the beaches, most of which seem to be permanently deserted, have become another element in my slow construction of the ideal imaginary life.

One afternoon, taking a break after two intensive weeks of language school, three of us were walking on a beach near Campos on Ikaria. We came to a whitewashed bench nestled into a curve on the backside of a house. Here we dozed and talked as the warm sun beat down on us with exactly the right fierceness, not enough to drive us into the shade, but to take off the chill of the wind whirling around our feet. After an hour or so a little old lady came along with shopping bags and opened the gate into the garden of her tiny house. She smiled when she saw us on her bench, and said something we couldn't understand, but which probably was a summons to come inside for a coffee. We looked at one another and decided to leave rather than accept her invitation, thus foregoing another opportunity for an intimate peek into island culture. We all felt mutually rude and guilty as we hurried off down the beach.

Maybe if we had been in the mountains . . . , but on the seashore there is an unspoken right to a kind of vegetable state of mind.

Yet later, on a different beach, I spent a great deal of time sitting cross-legged on top of a wall behind another small, whitewashed house. The wall served again as a boundary between house and sand. I sat facing sideways, so that with my peripheral vision I could see the windowless back of the house, and also the dappled shade of the trees under which we had dumped our beach gear, and where we spread our towels to indicate our temporary bit of territory for reading, eating, and changing clothes. I felt perfectly content here on the wall, whereas if I moved out onto the sand under the trees I was suddenly conscious of some anxiety and irritability. It was uncanny, almost as if I were a dowsing stick that dipped suddenly in the too-close proximity of water. But here, I dipped for House. So long as I could be near a house, I felt as if I belonged, as if it were okay to spend hours doing nothing, because this is where I *lived*, not just where I was "staying."

This particular house sweetly permitted me private rights to its story. It was deserted, standing with its back to the sea, and the front facing a beautiful meadow. A family had owned it for years, raising several generations of children, but finally all the children had gone away to live in Athens, leaving only an old couple, who had died within a week of one another. Nobody wanted to live there permanently any more, and although the grandchildren returned from time to time, the house was decaying, blandly and even with some small glee, anticipating the family's later regret. In the distance I saw an olive grove, and signs of gardens. Here must be the neighbors, who (when I took over the house) would drop by every morning, bringing olives, apricots, tomatoes and squash; I would provide coffee and flowers. We would sit in plastic chairs in the front yard, as if the sea were miles away, but aware of an extra richness from the constant possibility of walking on sand or taking a quick dip in the water. In the late afternoon I could carry my basket across seven fields, climb over a stone wall, go up a long hill, lift a latch in a gate, and I would be on a dirt road. After a mile this road would change to gravel, and soon I would come to a village with a market, a taverna, a church, and probably a small garage renting motorcycles.

I decided I could be perfectly happy here, alone, for a long time. Maybe if I were lucky, somebody would exile me here in a future life. I would only hope the sea did not become too loud on winter evenings.

Ikaria has natural, radioactive baths which have attracted pilgrims since ancient times. Most of these baths were once clustered around the village of Therma on the southwest coast, and most of them fell into the sea in a huge landslide at some unspecified time in history, probably no later than the end of the Roman Empire, thus bringing to an end Ikaria's most thriving ancient city. Nevertheless, in the 1920's Therma enjoyed a second heyday, when for a decade or so its springs were famous all over Europe, and the village flourished once more as a spa. The Depression, World War II, and the Greek Civil War effectively quashed this revival, and a second one has yet to occur.

A group of us went down to Therma one afternoon because Mihalis told us it wasn't normal, and we were intrigued. "It's different from all the other villages on the island," he said. "Nobody really lives there, everybody comes in to work from somewhere else."

Anita Sullivan

We drove to Therma via a narrow, switchback road, only this was the opposite of the way to Christos Raches; here you started on the mountaintop and came *down* to the village. Poppies bloomed beside the road, of such outrageous reds that we kept stopping to take pictures as we descended.

What remains of Therma now is a ghost town of 1920's-style hotels, mostly deserted. They line up in a mildly ghastly row along the tilted street, distinctly uninviting to someone seeking refreshment of body and mind. Nowadays the pilgrim, having just come down from the heights, might think of the warning at the gate of Dante's Hell, "Abandon hope all ye who enter here."

But it's not quite a ghost town. On this June afternoon there were a couple of tavernas open, and a really charming bed and breakfast villa overlooking the small harbor. Therma would be an ideal place to go if you wanted complete peace, seclusion, beauty—and maybe the odd splash in a medicinal pool. (The bath house in the plaza is open for business, offering serious medical therapies for a variety of ailments.) The setting for the town is quite beautiful, a deep cleft in the coastline, so that from the ridge above, the place glitters whitely like the enchanted coast city in the fairy tales. Even when you drive down the dusty and deserted main street, flowers are blooming everywhere. Some of the bougainvillea vines rise to twenty feet high and are brighter and more vivid than I have seen anywhere. Are their roots, by chance, dangling into an underground spring?

We spent the afternoon bathing in a sheltered pool by the sea. The locals directed us to the footpath along the cliff south of town, and told us we would eventually come to a pool far down among the steep rocks, a natural radioactive bath. They said it was okay to bathe there, so long as we didn't stay in too long. I swam up to the fissure in the cliff from which the yellow and green "medicine" oozed out, and stretched out my feet into it for a few seconds before I swam away. I am convinced my feet benefited from this brief therapy. The handful of tourists we met here were mostly Germans who had discovered the place, and returned faithfully every year.

On Ikaria you can bathe in the sea, but you can also go up the Chalares River from Nas and find your own private freshwater pool. I thought of Agamemnon, the ancient Greek hero who died in his bath. He was being paid back by his wife Clytemnestra for sacrificing their daughter Ifigenia at the beginning of the Trojan War. Her death allowed the winds to blow so the Greek ships could finally sail off to Anatolia, where ten years later a victory would be won against the mighty city of Troy, and Agamemnon would come home to cleanse himself from all the blood and gore of ten years earning his living as a general. After he had a nice warm soak, his wife threw a net over him to bind his mighty limbs, and then chopped off his head.

I decided to take the risk—I removed my clothes and climbed down into a sun-dappled pool for a soak. It was deep enough to cover me nicely, but not enough to swim. So I basked in a secluded dell far above the sea, not far from the sound of happy voices from other folks doing the same thing, some of them whole families with children, some of them probably pot-smoking hippies (the river has the reputation for attracting such). Ikaria is unusual in having at least this one year-round, mature river in addition to a fine collection of smaller, seasonal creeks. The Chalares bubbles out from springs high in the Atheras range, and falls over rocks, over huge boulders along its route, making small sandy beaches and allowing a lovely wedge of vegetation between the goat-infested hills.

Lying on my tummy on a warm rock I looked hard at the dirt, the tiny plants, the patterns of the shadows on the stones, and wondered, "Why do I have to travel thousands of miles do be doing this? What is there about this place that tells me for sure I am in Greece instead of in Oregon?" If I keep coming back here to Ikaria for a hit of the truly *different*, wherein does it lie? Do I have to run around with a magnifying glass studying the lichen on the rocks, and say, "Oh, we don't have any of that species in the United States?" How much has to be taken away, how much added, to any culture to make it "the same" as any other? In the parks here, in the town squares, the kids are wearing jeans and tee shirts and riding skateboards. People use computers, talk on cell phones, and live in ugly apartment buildings. The air is polluted all over the Mediterranean, so that the famous Greek light has been blotted out. You can get along fine here with only English. And though I have finally come to admit Mikis was right when he intuited that I was responding to the part of him that was typically Greek, I fell in love with what was *different* about that image—a way of moving, a light in the eyes. Whether this means Greece still is or ever was fundamentally different from the United States in all vital ways from the land to the souls of its people, or whether it just means the Greeks have a different way of revealing things, I don't really know or care.

Here something inside me said, "You're missing the main point." And I knew I was missing the main point, once again, by getting caught up in dualities. I can only trust that whatever is most vital and sustaining is gradually finding its way into my bones. Only

Ikaria

the brain stands between the music and the ears; like an old window frame over flowers, it can be lifted out in warmer weather for direct sun.

    I picked a handful of herbs by the roadside on my way back to Nas, which after returning home I sewed into a little green gauze bag and set in a bowl in my bathroom, so now I can imbibe intimations of Ikaria from the steam of my shower. The important things are the things you can't remember on purpose. Didn't Heraclitos say something like that?* I wish it weren't true, but it is, and we're stuck with it. You have to travel to remember.

* Heraclitos said, "Things keep their secrets."

Anita Sullivan

Life Beautiful

Η ζωή είναι ωραία, αλλα τα έχει με άλλον.
("Life is beautiful, but she's having an affair with somebody else.") — Greek proverb

In Ikaria it's tempting to jump to conclusions all the time. From very little evidence I could conclude the following: 1. Every small village on this island is populated chiefly by old people. 2. These old people live alone in small houses with very few modern conveniences. 3. The old people do all the work, tending the gardens, walking long distances to fetch water from the springs for their animals. 4. Their children and grandchildren all have professional jobs in Athens, nine hours away by ferry boat. 5. Their daily conversations with each other are very boring.

I could also conclude that the economy in Ikaria is improving, or getting worse. The population is growing, or not. Kyria Maria, the architect's wife in Campos, says times are better now, and the young people no longer leave the island for good when they finish high school, but they are coming back to buy houses and raise families. Yet, on the other hand, Yiannis the taxi driver says there is nothing for his five children to do when they grow up. Who is right?

Most of the people here survive by patching together a living. The baker is also an electrician; one of the local priests also runs a bar; and every family on the island has a little piece of land on which they raise vegetables and keep a few animals. Everybody is a shopkeeper, a landlord, a farm laborer or a repair-person, and often more than one of these. Versatility is the key to survival.

I think the Ikarians are really doing quite well, but they are tempted to see themselves as poor, needing to improve their way of life even more. After all, they have an ancient tradition of being the poorest island in the entire Aegean. This poverty has, in the past, been a source of pride, as well as a protection, politically and socially, from the bad aspects of the "outside world." Ironically, the Greek Government dumped its Communist exiles on Ikaria after the Second World War, and the island was so impressed with the behavior of these exiles that it adopted their philosophy, which very likely fit well with the self-image already in place—scruffy, maverick, self-sufficient . . . . So far as I can see, life on Ikaria today is about as close to ideal as humans have ever managed. Everyone seems to have enough, there is a close-knit community of healthy easy-going folks who know one another well, who gripe and bicker to keep themselves in emotional trim, and who are in touch with the outside world to avoid becoming stagnant. Someone needs to whisper the secret into their hearts: *"This is the definition of a good life that you would find, written in the big book if you were allowed to see it."*

    I walked one afternoon from Nas up to another of the several isolated monasteries that dot the island. All are deserted, all are small by European standards, and all exist in stunningly beautiful locations. This one is called, on the map, Evangelistrias. Three of the four monasteries on the island are listed on the official tourist map with the name "Evangelistrias," meaning "Annunciation," but that's only on the map. Already I know two of them as Theoktistis and Moni Mounte.

    This third "moni" also consists of a small church and some outbuildings. The larger of the buildings is simply a row of small rooms, each with a locked door and no window in the back, formerly monk's cells but now (peeking through the keyhole) used only for storage. The roof of the church is traditional island slate.

Anita Sullivan

One summer evening years ago, on my first trip to Greece, I had traveled by jeep with a group of people to a monastery high above the sea without knowing exactly where it was on the map, and now I wanted to make a private pilgrimage to check out my intuition that this particular "Evangelistria" was the same place. As soon as I set foot on the path by the orchard, past the old olive house, I felt the configuration of the land and the buildings wash over me with a biting familiarity. I had walked this ground before. The first time we had arrived in the thickness of early dusk, six of us in two jeeps, bouncing the switchbacks up the side of the cliff along the coast. An old man, the caretaker, had risen up from behind the church and immediately beckoned us into the small cell he was using as a kitchen. There he poured beer into an assortment of cups. The walls curved around us, whitewashed and lit by one small bright window. We were all silhouettes. Our guide on that trip was Pericles, a young curly-haired Greek patching together a living by renting jeeps and taking tourists on late-afternoon trips to remote spots on the island.

Remembering Pericles made me smile. He was, after all, the very first of the many young, handsome Greek men I met on my first trip to Ikaria, after Mikis had assured me that my love for him was based on a mere romantic stereotype. "But think of all the Greek men I have *not* fallen in love with!" I grinned, and began to count them on my fingers: Yiannis, Yiorgos, Mihalis, Angelos, Manolis . . . . There were quite a few. "Yes, it's not that I haven't been exposed to plenty of attractive guys who are also very Greek. Have I developed immunity at last, to Eros?" This was a new thought, and it made me feel light on my feet. I continued down the path between the monastery buildings.

Ikaria

Now, years later, the small kitchen was being used only to store boxes of Amstel (Dutch beer) and I wandered around the grounds in the company of a different old man, one who had given me a ride on his motor bike the last few hundred yards of the trip. I stumbled in weariness from the long hike and the intoxicating smells of wild herbs that saturate the air here. I took a photo of the enormous olive-crushing stone with the pestle lying in the middle, unchanged from five years before. It's just the right size for a Cyclops to work alone, standing twenty feet tall with his legs braced, groaning as he turns. Come to think of it, Ikaria still supports a stone-age culture, and why not? Stones are still forming somewhere deep inside the land and popping out at the surface, on and on forever, giving a sense that the stone is living in a way that nothing else can live. Certain of these stones—not all of them, but certain ones in walls, or in buildings, or like this olive stone—always make me squint and shiver, knowing I am witness to something very specific and well-rehearsed which I do not understand.

    I lit a candle in the church and sat quietly for awhile. Then on the stone bench in the small church yard I fought off the advances of the old man (a skill at which I have, sadly, become rather adept) until finally he got up with a grin and a shrug, and said his goodbyes, with an urgent reminder for me to snuff out the candles before I left because of the danger of fire.

The monastery garden was freshly tended, so someone was making use of the land here. It was, as usual, set out on a series of terraces, with a few rows of tomatoes coming up, and beans, grapes, lettuce, and onions. Nearby were olive, apricot, and fig trees, all the necessities for survival. I believe you could hardly walk half a mile anywhere on the island without finding a similar garden. I sat beside the little plot for a few minutes, imagining myself as the caretaker here. I have come to believe I would be totally happy just tending a garden like this, probably in the company of some other villagers, and spending the rest of my time writing, walking, and reading. What would our conversations be like? The Greeks have a reputation for being relentlessly philosophical. What kind of philosophy would we talk, we villagers, day after day together as we worked in our black rubber boots shifting the hoses around our small irrigated squares of garden, digging up rocks and hauling them away, pruning grapes, weeding, mounding dirt around our separate sections of vegetables?

With the old man on the motorcycle I got as far as the basic conversation, "Where are you from?" "What do you do?" "What is your name?" "Are you married?" "Do you have children?" After that, he started reaching for me and I kept pushing his hands away, until finally I stood up and walked over to the wall, shaking my head and saying "No!" His philosophy could not contemplate why a single woman would not want a little hanky-panky whenever she could get it. End of conversation.

Back at the hotels, the managers, the tour guides, the motorcycle rental agents, the tourist agents, the restaurant owners—all the Greek men who interact with tourists—if you start talking a little Greek with them, it's not long before you push their "philosophy" button. They start sounding like Zorba, with the philosophy "Live totally in the moment, because you only live once." My friend Pamela says whenever a Greek man starts talking like that to her she just laughs and tells him to quit. "Don't give me any of that stuff." she says, and he usually laughs and ruefully admits it is a line he has gotten used to spieling off.

So, what are the choices? When you finish the "usual conversation" of finding out name, age, matrimonial status, place of origin, kind of work—what then, what else is there to talk about, ever?

Pamela is seriously thinking of buying land here, of building herself a traditional stone house. Not even the locals do this any more: breaking stone into building-block sizes is bone-hard labor that must still be done by hand, and skilled stone masons are scarce. It's easier to use the ubiquitous concrete. And yet, though she has been coming to Greece for 20 years and has an expressed desire to live here permanently, she can't quite make the final decision to do it. "You should not move to a Greek island until you have spent a winter there," Mikis told me one night in the Beanery in Corvallis when I was overflowing with philhellenic enthusiasm.

"What do you do here in the winter?" I asked Yiannis one day.

"Same thing we do in the summer," he said, much to my surprise.

"What do you mean?"

"I mean we stay out all night with friends," he smiled. "Go hunting up in the hills."

Some Ikarians come to the island only during the high tourist season in summer, or they live here six or seven months each year. Others leave frequently for trips to Athens, or to visit friends in Europe or the United States. Each person finds a way to come to terms with this place, which more than normally masquerades as paradise.

On my way back from the monastery in the blazing sun, into my fourth hour of walking, I came upon an old woman trudging along in the same direction, carrying two enormous pails of water. She was wearing a dark dress with a pattern of small white flowers, a sweater, a kerchief holding back her hair, socks and loafer-like shoes.

I asked if I could help her, and she gratefully handed me one bucket. We had the standard conversation, and then we went up the side of a hill so she could water her goats. She told me to wait at the bottom and she would meet me further down the road so we could stop off at her house for a "neraki" (small glass of water). But I went on up the hill with her and sat among the gorse bushes while she talked to her goats in her high old-lady voice for half an hour or so.

As we were back on the road again walking towards her house in the tiny village, she asked me a question. "Life, is it good, do you think?" she asked me. It was a simple question, which I don't think I was mistaken in hearing. She asked it clearly, as if she really wanted my opinion on the subject. So, I said "Yes, I think life is good." And I nodded my head, remembering later that nodding can mean just the opposite in Greece; a sudden lifting of the chin into the air means a very strong "No!" But maybe she had met enough tourists by now to know how silly we are with our gestures, rolling our heads around in wild abandon. I asked her where she was born, and she said Epirus, which by Greek standards is very far away. Her husband is dead; she has no relatives left in Epirus to go back to. Her exile continues. "Do you like it here in Ikaria?" I asked, and she shrugged and rolled her eyes. "What can you do?" she said. And I had some small inkling of why she had asked me if life was good.

Still, the question stunned me. I have no idea what she really meant. Was this a true bit of philosophy? Philosophy, after all, in the Socratic sense, can be a mutual exploration of the nature of reality, a quest for truth. Did she really want to know? My god, what if she really did want to know? I have never had anyone ask me that question before, or anything close. But maybe I misunderstood her. Maybe her question was just part of the standard conversation, an old Greek peasant woman's version of irony, or fatalism, or even humor. For the present, I prefer to remain stunned.

Anita Sullivan

Jasmine

Everywhere I go, Greece wounds me.
George Seferis

Smells open up the world and make it truly round. It's not only their ability to unleash memories in a way that makes you totally helpless, like an elephant being twirled slowly around on the fingertip of a child—sometimes a piquant fragrance won't be familiar at all, but in its presence you will suddenly notice that you are very much alive, a feeling you weren't even aware had once again slipped away from you.

I don't know if jasmine is for memory, as rosemary is meant to be. Gabriel Garcia Marquez, in his novella *La Hojarasca* (*Leaf Storm*), has the Colonel plant a jasmine vine in memory of his dead wife, because "he'd read somewhere that when a loved one dies we should set out a bed of jasmine to remember her every night." Jasmine, which I love, never fails to remind me of Greece.

I am sitting on a park bench in Rethymnon, Crete, a few hours before I get on a bus for the airport to start my journey back to Oregon. Behind the bench are oleander bushes in bloom. If I look up I can see palm trees high above the other trees in the park, and the air is filled with the chirr of something like locusts.

I am staring at the packed dirt in front of me and checking out my soul by running my thoughts backwards over it, gently, carefully. The night before, a Greek schoolteacher I met in a restaurant had walked me back to my hotel and forced himself into my room. It was 2:00 in the morning, I didn't want to shout; it wasn't worth it. So, we had sex, and it was not traumatic, only boring and strenuous and humiliating. Now, the next morning I am walking around feeling absolutely rotten, much worse than I thought I would feel. After all, I'm in my middle 50's; I'm supposed to be mature enough to handle a case of date rape. But though I've been naïve about trusting men before, I don't seem to have learned anything or developed any survival skills during my many trips to Greece; therefore, I must be an innately weak person, totally unfit for this land, where strength of character must be firmly and outwardly expressed. Last night I assumed my stony indifference would substitute for shouting and pushing, and would serve as my own emotional insulation as well. But here in the cold morning light I see that behavior as my usual rationale for a deep unwillingness to risk confrontation. Now, overwhelmed by the emotional aftermath of last night's sordid event, I am wondering how this will fall out in memory. If I am truthful, if I go over and over the previous evening, minute by minute like a detective, to absolve myself of blame, will I still be able to hold onto my illusion about Greece? Will I still have a totally irrational passion for the place? Will this indiscretion make me finally lose the original momentum that propelled me here, a momentum resulting from an ill-conceived (almost illicit) passion for a man much younger than myself? I don't truthfully know where that original love for Mikis has gone. When I am in Greece I can feel it somewhere inside me, like a malaria germ perhaps, in the traditional, ancient Greek sense of love as "Eros," an illness of both body and spirit that periodically pricks humans into a state of heightened awareness they can not forswear. Other ways of loving I have been able to experience gracefully at home. But as part of my personality now, I count on a secret, familiar, unfocussed passion that I have nurtured during my many trips to Greece; I don't believe it is either good or bad, but in some way it keeps me not just emotionally, but spiritually balanced. Last night's stupid mistake on my part, if it threatens that balance, could be dangerous.

As my new acquaintance and I walked through the streets after midnight, away from the little place in the Old Town where the music was gently lyrical in the traditional Cretan style, we passed a wall with jasmine in bloom, sending its delicate, secret scent out into the night. Yiorgos reached over to pick a blossom and hand it to me. "You like jasmine?" he said in Greek, his dark eyes shining with happiness, and I said yes I did. We might have been lovers, for just that one moment.

This trip to Greece has too many secrets. I am bound by silence, because most of my experiences have been too small and strange to tell. When you travel in a land where you do not know the language well, you walk around inside a helmet of silence, which can, in the long term, have the same sort of healing power that silence always has, not because there is no noise around you, but because you are not *saying* anything, and this muteness begins to turn you back into an honest human being again. That means something resembling moss, or bone. If I ask myself, "How do you really feel about last night?" and if I hear myself articulating an answer, it is just as if I have told someone else a secret; then I have to ask again, and receive a slightly different answer. But it is in *not asking* that I will regain the balance I need.

So, here I am in Rethymnon walking around Old Town looking at the varieties of marble arching above double doors of magnificently differing natural woods, rounded at the top to nest into the marble. Such doors always make me weak with desire to turn the knob and walk in, because I know inside will be a low passageway

Ikaria

leading to an open garden where vines are blooming along balustrades, and someone is pouring wine, and there is water running over stone. I walk along thinking subliminally about how many different shades of yellow the Italian way of building always produces, happily stepping out of the path of motorcycles, and wondering if I love this part of town so much why don't I just go to Italy instead of Greece?

Two days ago I was up on the walls of the old Venetian citadel that rises above one corner of this lovely small city in northern Crete. The walls are a pinkish color, which seems strange at first until you realize that, of course, this building came directly out of the soil, and is linked to the soil still, even though now the two of them no longer have exactly the same chemistry. The buildings on the campus of the University of Wyoming in Laramie are that way too, and when I saw the fortress at Rethymnon I had the same initial jolt that I remember in Laramie, where I was visiting my brother ten years ago. He was dying of cancer, and the whole family was spending a week with him, doing whatever he felt like doing, going for long walks in the snow or sitting in coffee shops letting our conversation drift back and forth from the profound to the trivial. For some reason the strange pinkish color of the buildings hit me then like a pain, and now that I see it again in Greece, I think it must have been because it forced me to have an attitude about beauty, in a time and place when I merely wanted to be numb.

"Everywhere I travel, Greece wounds me," said George Seferis, who spent much of his adult life in exile from his country. Now I approach the Venetian walls, which swell with the addition of my old memories, and I am pre-disposed to tears. I snap pictures of the city spread out below, its red-tiled roofs, the clarity of the contrasts between greens of the trees, low mountains around the edges, and the white, white walls of the houses. I sit on the wall and breathe the dust. The walls are crumbling back to dust, quietly, beyond the attention of the spiffy new city below. Here in the crevices where cannons used to rest their heavy chins, I see a bee crawling belly-deep in the powdery stuff. He is working very hard at dying, standing up on his front legs, rubbing his rear legs together, and then toppling to one side before he starts over again. I sit beside him for awhile and wonder why he is putting so much energy into this sort-of dance. Years ago I would have believed my sympathy would go out in a small wave like something physical, to let him know a fellow creature was beside him at the end. But now I no longer believe that. This is another secret we hold under our tongues, we creatures of earth, that we die alone. My brother told me this.

In Assisi years ago, above the Umbrian plain, listening to the tolling of the bells in the evening, I could sense other people's memories in me, and a deep nostalgia for this place that I had never seen before. It is like slipping into a parallel life, a place your bones find sweetly familiar even though your brain can't quite recall. I think all true ecstasy is based on this phenomenon, a kind of cellular familiarity that happens only in certain places, with certain people, and not much more often than a lunar eclipse. On this trip to Greece it is not happening. I keep putting myself into the right position, like the actress holding her pose before the camera, waiting for the rush of the blood to the head, the mild nausea, which indicate the onset of rapture. But instead, I continue to be infected with an attitude of normalcy.

Ikaria

There I was, a few days ago, sitting on a terrace at the ruins of Phaestos in the south of Crete, sipping a frappe exactly where Henry Miller had drunk a mavrodaphne with the old Greek caretaker back in the late 1930's. I should have been mist-drunk with the blue mountains, the rubble of King Minos' old city, the cloud shadows on the fields in the valley below; and I felt nothing but irritation at the flies, worry that the haze in the valley might be pollution.

To the blind heart, feeling in the dark, a country can be very like a person. You run some of the same risks; going back for a second look you may find the country has become more demanding, more dangerous. In Iraklion I was poring over a map outside the archaeological museum, hoping to figure out how to get to the bus station for Phaestos. A slender, middle-aged man in a dress shirt and neat gray slacks asked if he could help. He led me on a rapid ten-minute walk through twisting streets to my destination, which I probably would have taken half a day to find. We agreed to meet for a coffee the next morning in the museum gardens. After that we spent the morning walking around the harbor, talking about life and literature and love—all those big subjects which, to my huge delight, it seems the Greeks still have a yen to figure out. On the way back from the harbor my new friend stopped briefly at a souvenir shop and insisted that I pick out some memento of our time together. I chose a little black Minoan vase, about four inches high. "I will set this right next to my telephone," I told him, "and so every day I will think of you." When we said good-bye, his eyes were full of tears. And I do have the little vase next to my phone, years later, and I do think of him sometimes. Traveling,

Anita Sullivan

as Seferis says, wounds you. But oddly enough there is some comfort in his little poem, "The Jasmine":

> *In dusk*
> *or in shine*
> *it stays white –*
> *the jasmine.*

Ikaria

Merely Voice

Would it were anything but merely voice!
The No King cried who after that was King,
Because he had not heard of anything
That balanced with a word is more than noise.
   William Butler Yeats

At age eight I almost took a vow of silence. Like many children at this age, I had developed my own code regarding just and unjust acts on the part of parents, and when my mother said, "Be quiet, Anita," suddenly and loudly on the sidewalk in front of our house, I felt she had resorted to an unjust method of dealing with my behavior. She had destroyed a delicate balance by speaking to me publicly about a private family matter.

"Ok," I wanted to shout back, *"I'll never say another word the rest of my life!"*

Instead, I blinked and watched my future suddenly unroll before me as if I were drowning. "That's an awful long time to be quiet," I thought. And in what was probably the first cautious decision of my life, I opted for immediate humiliation instead of deferred humiliation, and kept my mouth clamped shut.

I met Mikis for the last time on a sunny July afternoon as he was riding slowly across campus on his bicycle. He could not avoid, out of politeness, stopping to ask about my recent trip to Greece. "So, you did not have to speak nearly as much Greek as you feared you would?" he said, his eyes laughing. "Right," I answered, and that was the end of our relationship. To himself, he was probably saying, "She met other Greek men so now I'm off the hook as the romantic ideal." To myself I was saying, "You're wrong, Mikis, I didn't meet a single man anything like you, and I will never forget you for the rest of my life."

Now I wonder if keeping my childhood vow might have been a better way to go. I would have become like the young woman in Jane Campion's film and book *The Piano*, who first would not speak, then finally could not. Years of voluntary muteness, like water on stone, eroded the sharp urgency of her need to rise and make voice, until—her entire being finally became flat enough or weak enough to slip back into the native land of silence that at some cellular level we all yearn for. As a piano tuner, I spend hours with my mouth shut and my ears open, exploring mysterious resonances that the sound of my own voice would destroy. Muteness would not be much of a handicap in my livelihood. And as a poet, I long ago discovered—or more accurately I should day *decided*—that the most important things can't be said with words. What we say in silence to everything we recognize and care for, with or without name, is all the fuel the universe truly ever needs to continue spinning on its way. For what do we need to be all the time building towers of babble?

"Would it were anything but merely voice!" cried the king in a poem by William Butler Yeats. Presumably the old monarch was frustrated because the strength of meaning in words may be enormous, yet the physical power of voice is weak, useless as a weapon when it emerges from the throat. Alas, the vocal chords of humans are puny, nowhere near as strong as our inventing and devious minds.

Nevertheless, there is all the distance in the world between pulling a trigger or not. The same with the human voice, in that nether land between speech and silence. Any vow of silence I would take would leave me free to roam this space, and I would defy His Majesty to say that voice does not have, in this realm, a power equal to cannons.

One night, scarcely twenty four hours after returning from my first trip to Greece, I drove forty miles to Eugene to hear Bach's "B Minor Mass." I had purchased the ticket months earlier, knowing I would be at the peak of severe jet lag on this night. "Sleep took me," is what the Greeks say when they are late for work due to oversleeping. I would not want Sleep to take me on my way home in the dark. But I'll never miss a performance of this work if I am able to attend.

As I settled into my seat in the third row of the lower balcony, a portly and courtly gentleman in the seat next to me struck up a conversation. On the other side was his grandson, who was learning about Bach. We read our programs side by side, and talked about our favorite sections of this beloved piece. After awhile, unable to stifle my jet-lag yawning, I confided that I had just come back from Greece. Turns out he had been a cryptographer in Piraeus during World War II; they chose him because he had studied ancient Greek for two years in college. He asked if I had seen the latest translation of *The Odyssey* and said he was just re-reading Ovid's *Metamorphosis* which I had read for the first time about a year ago. It was a very civilized and pleasant conversation.

I think it might have been during the "Laudamus Te" of the "Gloria," or perhaps my memory is not quite accurate, since that is one of my own weak spots, where tears come every time. Beside me the old gentleman was clenching his hands together in his lap. "Oh, God!" I heard him whisper. "Oh, God, please, no!"

This was a totally private comment; I was not meant either to hear or to remember it. I broke out in goose bumps. He was not speaking words for me or for any other human; he was saying something secret, and thus inscrutable. Here was a different dimension, a place for pure voice and no ears, like the tree in the forest falling in isolation. This is impossible, I grew even dizzier. Where am I?

A vow of silence would not exclude such small desperate whispers as the one this man made. It would not need to exclude the "Oh!" which breaks from your mouth when beauty rushes too suddenly out of the void and hits you in the solar plexus. A hummingbird hovers outside the window for three glorious seconds while you are drinking tea. You round the corner in the museum and are confronted for the first time in your life with an original canvas of one of Monet's "Water Lilies." You are making love. What we say at times like this is more related to silence than to language, I believe. Or at least, when the knife of distinction cuts, such spontaneous outbursts will be found to be part of a great headland, firmly attached to an ancient continent. It may be the same continent in which lie the person-hoods of every single human who has died since the beginning of time. Here prevails a kind of pulsing dark. This is what I mean by the silence of the vow I could not take.

The human voice, even when speaking, can be an equivalent of silence if people don't understand what is being said. This non-communication can happen for a variety of reasons, of course: inattention, illness, emotional stress, ignorance of the subject matter, or when the language being spoken is foreign to one of the listeners. I experienced that forcefully one morning on a Greek ferry, when I settled into a seat by the window somewhat apart from the bulk of the passengers, who were chattering loudly in competition with the television at the front of the room. Weak sunlight filtered through the thick, salt-blurred windows onto my lap, and I leaned my head back and closed my eyes. The voices—speaking a language I have some familiarity with—started to take on a rhythm which I identified as totally unfamiliar, even though I had heard it many times before. A cold realization came to me: these people were not only speaking a language I did not understand, they were speaking a language I *could not* understand, even if it were suddenly translated. Translated into what? For once I had lost the usual idea of *what people are doing with their voices*. For a few moments, in my dazed state, I had an insight into the nature of human vocal discourse which broadened it from language into something huge, almost insect-like, as if the ordinary Greek families talking across the aisle from me were broadcasting atomic resonance frequencies, or as if they were exchanging a semi-patterned hissing and humming fashioned from the migration of their individual cells through the organs of their bodies. This was not speech, it was merely voice, and it struck me full-force as if it were a hurricane. Later, thinking about what had happened, I realized that any sound, when it swells into an optimum state like that, or goes on long enough, can be equated with silence. My problem was that I never could let go of the sound, only the meaning, and the result was a small, temporary insanity.

Memory, too, can be a kind of selective silence when it fails, or is rejected on purpose. I am thinking of my mother, who has developed an Alzheimer's-like illness in her middle 80's. Now her memory is like a basket, with holes and solid places interwoven. She laughs about it, shrugs, wears leopard-skin tights, blows kisses to the gentlemen playing chess on the veranda of the Activities Center. All the jokes she carefully saved for years on scraps of paper and stuffed into manila envelopes, which I never knew about, now she can read them over and over again, for hours. She will never be at a loss for a good laugh. This is her voice, ringing out of the silence. I sit on the sofa talking to her, and wonder, "What do we need so much memory for? We humans are such a bunch of busybodies. If we just re-invented the wheel a few thousand more times, we would be so much more beneficial to the universe. That's what birds do, and the alligators, and the trees. They choose their words more carefully than we do."

"I was brought up . . ." my mother begins again, at 7:30 in the evening with a glass of bourbon beside her on the coffee table, the table that she inlaid with tile thirty years ago. "Mother and Dad really suffered during the Depression. Dad had plenty of patients, but they couldn't afford to pay him. Sometimes he would make only two dollars in an entire month. We ate a lot of scrambled eggs and vegetables, which people left on the porch. Mother started an art school to make ends meet." I've heard the story a hundred times. My mind drifts. I am listening to her voice, trying to engrave it on my memory, against the terrible silence when it stops.

Ikaria

Honey and Wine

The hive is the highest caste,
well of amber that feeds the rhythm
of bees. Breast of the countryside
trembling with scent and sound.

Honey is the epic of love,
matter of the infinite.
Pained soul and blood of flowers
condensed through another spirit.
                from "The Song of Honey" by Frederico
                Garcia Lorca, translated by Frank Pascoe

In the end I had no choice but to make a special trip to Ikaria about the bees. Nobody laughed at me when I gave as my excuse for traveling twenty eight hours straight, the chance of catching a glimpse of some ancient hives. Ted came along, my new husband. I was excited to be able to show him around on his first trip to Greece. We stopped in Luxembourg on the way over, to visit Jackie, one of my old language schoolmates, and we traded news—Sophia, the former student who danced with the postman at Drousoulas is now living in Athens and about to have a baby—Toula, the owner of a little restaurant outside Evdilos has published a book of poetry—Yiannis is still not married, but his parents have become reconciled—Nikos, the old violinist, is alive but not well—Mihalis and Ifighenia closed the school early this year, and have reverted to being just good friends—Pamela is thinking of buying some land in Kato Proespera and building a traditional stone house—the airport has not turned the island into a tourist trap—Ikaria might start growing wine grapes again after 2000 years.

Anita Sullivan

On Ikaria the bees are enormous. Among the hillside herbs in spring the droning is a constant thunder at the bottom of the air, so that if you did not see them, you would swear an odd new weather had set itself up in this place. The bee-sound is loud enough to drown out the sea a hundred feet down, which only goes "swish" on a calm day. I believe this black humming might be strong enough to sustain me if I were to leap into it like a circus clown missing her trapeze.

Ikarians are beekeepers and have been from the beginning of their history. High in the Atheras mountain range (peak is 1,042 meters) rows of bright blue bee houses dot the rocky fields beside the island's one main road. Ikarian honey is sold in local grocery stores and has a taste as rich and complex as any good wine. In fact, the honey is better than the wine by a long shot, since local wine is strictly an acquired taste, and if Dionysos stopped in Ikaria first on his way from Ionia to the Greek mainland, he must have left behind one of his earlier recipes. Ikarian bees feed on the many wild herbs and flowers that cover the hillsides in spring, summer and fall. They are not confined to one or two flowers, nor likely can they be restricted in their feeding; the piquancy and wildness of the resulting honey is splendid.

It has occurred to me to compare birds and bees, the good and the beautiful, soul and spirit, the inside and the outside, being and doing. Because the differences between these things are different differences. And when I lie on my back under a pine tree halfway up a long slope listening to bees, I begin to wonder if there is any distinction between a huge difference and no difference at all.

Bees, for example, can hear. Like humans, they rely upon the motion of air to convey information. But we, with our larger ears, hear by responding to oscillating pressure waves or "sound waves" as we have come to call them. Bees' tiny receiving organs lie at the hinge of their antennae, and they apparently miss the pressure waves entirely, but instead are set off by air particles when they are not gathered into pressure waves, but are nevertheless making a regular motion pattern. For us, it would be as if we were able to "hear" the conductor's hand as it waved back and forth in front of the orchestra, instead of the instruments. A fine distinction? It depends on what your attention is drawn to. If "hearing" can be two distinct ways of sifting the common air, what else might be going on in our universe?

In Athens once, in the heart of the Plaka, I stopped to look at a man dressed as a woman, standing totally still and posing before a crowd. He was wearing a white dress and his face and arms and legs were dusted with white, to give the impression that he was made of marble (or at least that's what I decided later). He stood in a graceful, stylized pose, arms bent and palms up, head tilted slightly back, eyes opened wide but seeing nothing. People paused for awhile to look at him on their way past the Church of the Transfiguration of Christ, before which he stood motionless, as if he were an incarnation of one of the icons painted on the walls inside. We watched him for minutes at a time, and hardly saw him blink. There was a hat or something on the ground in front of him; he was performing for money. Motion and stillness. Male and female. Statue and living human. How long can a man stand in the noonday sun before he moves? Why did he not dress as St. Michael or St. George, instead?

Anita Sullivan

    Geographically, Ikaria is located precisely at the boundary of two island complexes, the Cyclades and the islands of the Eastern Aegean. This location gives a duality to the landscape, for Ikaria exhibits certain climatic, topographical, and biological features from both regions. At the same time the island contains several species of plants and one species of lizard that are found nowhere else in the world; as if the donkey caught between two bales of hay decided to sit down and eat the oats hanging around his neck. The landscape alternates between lush and dry, since several small streams and one river have water year round, while on the other hand much of the island is treeless and covered with huge granite rocks. If you didn't mind the thorns, you could bound down the side of a slope above the sea in May and your feet would strike a different herb at every step: lavatera, lavender, curry, wild pea, vetch, wild radish, rumex, mullein, fennel, rosemary, prickly pear, komaria, heather, lentisk, peony, digitalis, runemark, roripa, and symphytum. Then you could go back to your stone cave-house under a boulder, crouch in the doorway and look out across a high desert dotted with thistles and nettles, sucking perhaps on a husk of carob or a wild cherry.

    The word "Icaria," before Icarus secured a monopoly on it, involves the blending of two Kings. Their stories, like two fiery streams of lava, converge in the age of myth and plunge together into the future. Icarius was the father of Penelope, who married Odysseus. At one time he was a co-ruler in Sparta, and is best known as the first human taught by Dionysos to make wine. His first wine recipe was so strong that it made the shepherds to whom he offered it *see double*—and convinced they were bewitched they murdered him.

Ikaria

The other Icarus ("Icarus" instead of "Icarius," a fine distinction) was King of the Carians in Asia Minor, a historic race of pre-Greeks famous for being excellent pirates. Ironically, today's Ikarians sometimes call themselves "Carians" for short, but this (they assure me) does not mean that the Carians had anything at all to do with the name of their island. The two Kings and their legends joined sometime in the sixth century B.C., at which time, the name "Ikaria" had occurred in a tiny fragment of Homer's *Iliad* to refer to the island where the waves were enormous because of the wind. Icarius, Penelope's father, found out the hard way that wine imposes a double-seeing lens, especially when drunk improperly, that is, without an equal measure of water. Ikaria is the first island where Dionysos paused in his great awakening migration west founding the city of Drakanon on the island's northeastern tip, and Icarus was buried on Ikaria by his father, after he fell drowned in the sea, drunk with joy.

Everywhere I have traveled in Greece I have seen double-facing birds, sometimes more like two eagles, sometimes two peacocks. Nobody is able to tell me what they mean. I have sketched them inside small churches, seen them welded into wrought iron on fences, run into their images on the walls of houses in back streets of villages. In a church in Galissa, on Syros, resides a pair of brass peacocks with long sinuous necks curving in the shape of a C, touching at the back but curving away from each other like a mirror image. Yet their bodies are faced inward so that their claws clasp one another, as if the top halves didn't know what the bottom halves were doing. This is in a Catholic church, with a statue of Mary and Jesus on either side. When the birds are eagles their bodies are joined at the shoulder and tail, so that the result is like a very wide bird with two heads looking away from one another. "They are the double-axe of the Minoans," one person insisted. Myself, I believe the birds are angels in another form; they may be the same as the angel inside many Greek churches which shows up as a face encircled by a double set of wings. The birds are doubled because the angels have two sets of wings, and this in turn signifies a plethora, a hint of the infinite without going too far in that direction. It is not the pattern that shifts, but the symbols; so you have a great motion atop a great stillness.

In Oregon, it was Pamela who first told me about the old beehives. "They are up on the hillsides, arranged like little villages. They look like Greek urns turned over on their sides." I did some research and discovered this is the oldest hive shape in recorded history. And in Greece, very few of are left, mostly on the mainland.

Beekeeping began—so far as the historical record tells us—in Egypt around 2400 B.C., likely even earlier. The Egyptians took their beekeeping seriously; the visual record shows busy groups of workers smoking hives, extracting honey, and there is no question but that their hives were cylindrical pots. The ancient government in Egypt had a system for grading honey, and would stamp the clay containers with seals according to one of four degrees of purity. As late as the 1980's, the majority of hives used in Egypt were still the old, cylindrical pottery ones rather than the square wooden boxes that have since become nearly universal.

When Ted and I arrived in Armenistis, I believe half the people on the island already knew I was writing a book and that there would be a chapter about the old beehives. The fact that these old hives still exist on Ikaria had come to symbolize for me the blend of old and new which gives the island such charm and strength. In fact, it may be that Ikaria has skipped altogether the era of mass tourism with its chain hotels and package tours and instead is at the forefront of the more recent eco-tourism movement: small groups of people who like to blend as much as possible with the native environment, cultural and natural, as they make their independent explorations.

"A week won't be enough." I had wailed to Ted when we were planning this trip. "In Greece you don't rush things. I can't just waltz in and say, here I am, take me to your hives!"

But the Ikarians fooled me again. On the first morning the subject came up as four of us sat in the hotel lobby drinking coffee. Manolis, the hotel owner, smiled and waved his hand at a tall, cylindrical urn behind my back, filled with dried grasses and flowers. "This is one of the hives," he said, and then banged his forehead with his hand. "I can't remember the name."

"Oh, it's not kypseli?" I asked. This was the word I had memorized, along with a whole list of other handy beekeeping words from my dictionary, most of which turned out to be useless. People never actually use the words they're supposed to.

"No, kypseli is the word for the modern, square wooden beehive." And Manolis disappeared into his office to make a phone call for me, tracking down the right name. I couldn't help but think, "Now we are in the age of square hives. Years ago they were circular. What does this mean?"

"Chastriá," he said triumphantly, giving me the plural form and writing it down for me in Greek and in Greek English, (xi, alpha, sigma, tau, ro, iota, alpha). I later discovered this word is not in my enormous Greek-to-Greek dictionary, unless it begins with a gamma. Maybe this is a sign of an Ikarian dialect version of the name for ancient beehive? Pamela, who is spending two months here to research the ancient Ikarian dialect, might be able to find out for sure.

The week was flying by, and we still hadn't gone up into the hills to find the beehives. "Fate is at work," I told Ted Wednesday night. We had to leave Sunday morning to start our two-day trip back to Oregon. "If I don't find the hives by Sunday morning, I'm *staying here.*" We had idled away our time visiting the school, visiting Thea and Eleas at their little restaurant and rooming house in Nas where I once stayed a week, visiting Mihalis at the school, meeting two new friends and going up to their castle on the hill above the village of Ksanthi, talking to Yiannis on the porch of his parents' bar. "Do you remember the time you played the violin?" he smiled as he brought us our coffee. Koula asked me about my two sons. She always remembers that I, too, have a son in his 30's who is not married, and we both share a secret worry about our boys which is similar (I can feel it), and which is one of those inexplicable mother things.

I was amassing information about honey and bees. Nobody else on the island had any special interest in the old hives, or even in the new ones. But they were all very willing to help me out. Mihalis said there used to be a bunch of beehive doorway stones lying around his grandfather's house, where he lives in Arethousa. These stones have been hewn into roughly circular shape to serve as covers for the front end of the hives, with a little notch on one side for the bees to go in and out. Each stone cover was propped up against the circular opening with a long, skinny rock, making a kind of ad-hoc doorway. Even though the smaller, bottom end of the clay pot was open, it was wedged firmly into the back of the hollow space dug out in the hillside for the hive.

Angelos told us about the kinds of honey. "This time of year you get heather honey," he explained. Yes, we had noticed that the entire island was a mass of furiously blooming lavender heather. "This honey is not sweet, and it comes out looking like a beige bar of soap, not very appetizing. You have to melt it, and at first it tastes a bit like medicine. But if you put some of this honey on a piece of toast in the morning, you will feel full of energy for the rest of the day."

There is also the worm honey, which Ikarian honey-producers have been trying to live down. "I can give you the gory details," said Angelos with a grin. The Ikarians call it, euphemistically, "pine honey," and it's made from a kind of worm-shit. The ubiquitous island pine trees have a parasite, a tiny worm-like creature, which eats the bitter bark, and then in March they emerge from the bark and the trees are covered with a white excretion from their bodies. This happens to be sweet, and the bees love it. They lick it, cover themselves with it, and turn it into "pine honey." Unfortunately like retsina, the famous pine-flavored Greek wine, pine honey is an acquired taste, much less acquired than the taste for retsina.

On Friday we went up to the hives at last. We drove till the dirt road became a path, and walked past a small house with a collection of square wooden hives piled around it. Soon the path started to go up, and between rocks and grass and trees we saw beekeepers in full costume, holding hoses. They were probably smoking out hives. We just kept on walking, right through their private property, the way you can do in Greece and nobody comes out with a shotgun to chase you off.

"There they are!" cried Pamela, and pointed to some piles of rocks off on the hillside. Ted and I knew we would never have seen them by ourselves. A little "village" of stone rectangles each stuffed with a clay cylinder. Like round pegs in square holes. "Like an Indian cemetery," Angelos had said, quoting what some visitors had exclaimed on their first sighting.

We wandered around among the ancient hives. It was quiet, not even the sound of bees could be heard here. "All the self-respecting bees have decamped to the new hives," we decided. There they have part of their work already done for them. No longer do they have to come into a dark chamber with only a few score lines along the walls to give them a foothold. Since the late nineteenth century when the modern self-spacing, removable square frames were invented with their pre-configured wax and plastic combs, the bees are able to devote more of their energy to making honey, and less to making wax. "The bees, after all, have to make a perfect hexagon from scratch," Angelos pointed out. "It's not easy, even for them. They have to figure it out every time." We all laughed, wondering how long it might take for instinct to "forget" how to construct this fundamental shape of sacred geometry without a protractor, without starting with a point and drawing a circle around it, as we would have to do. If bees are making honey in square hives, with pre-configured hexagons, what is the world coming to?

Later we went up into a pine forest to find the second group of hives, and lay on the dry pine needles for awhile. "This is a holy place," we said to one another, and we could feel it. The deserted bee houses exuded a kind of quiet which was different from any other I have ever known. We peeked inside one or two of them, carefully, just in case someone was still living there. But they were all empty. No little dark bodies clustered around the entry holes. To either side of us fields of heather bloomed, and we could hear bees humming there. No doubt they took their heavy burden of pollen back across the valley to the new apartment complex on the other side.

It is a blessing to feel—for a brief time—light, beautiful, and stunned by love. It seems as if the periods of loving, like resonances or like orbits, have been increasing as I grow older. Perhaps, if they become constant, thus no longer periods at all, I would die. That could be a goal, not to die until they do.

The next day, when I took Ted up to the Monastery of the Madonna of the Annunciation on the road above Proespera, we noticed that all the candles in the tiny chapel were made of beeswax. Angelos had told us it took the Greeks about 30 years to realize the paraffin candles were turning the walls of their churches black, and sullying the beautiful icons and frescos. Beeswax does not catch fire, it just melts.

Before we left Ikaria, Pamela presented us with a jar of local honey, made in one of the square hives. I wish it were possible to taste some old honey, from the cylindrical Chastriá with their doors of island slate. I'd like to think I could tell the difference between the two.

Anita Sullivan

Epilogue

About a year ago I came to a kind of realization: *Each life is the slow, watchful, continuous, and (ultimately) cherished crumbling of a powerful heart.*

But Pamela wrote a letter from Ikaria, where she is spending a long autumn researching the ancient island dialect: "What I am discovering is slowly breaking my heart. The old way of life here is ending. A threshold has been crossed and everyone knows it."

So, I found it necessary to expand my realization. What about the heart of an island? It is not the same as a human heart. I can shield myself from excess pain (premature crumbling, if you will) by drinking sparingly from Lethe, the river of forgetfulness. Acting with love and care, I can thus make myself a more useful and balanced person. I have some control over the direction and nature of my days, and especially how much I am obliged to know about the many significant and terrible actions taking place in the world. But an island is helpless before its shapers: weather, custom, a horde of individuals each chipping her and his life out of the rock. Goats and television, fire and the internet, concrete and stone.

It is the integrity of the human heart that, in the end, must sustain the island's heart: like the rock retaining walls built eons ago to hold wine grapes, to hold the people as they walked back and forth to their houses scattered among the steeps of the landscape. How do we humans each keep our own hearts intact through a lifetime? Socrates told us (so far as I understand) we are each responsible for *finding out* the essential things we don't yet know. Our island waits for us to do this. Its rhythms shape us, soothe us, incite

Ikaria

us, nourish us—but ultimately, the island depends on the beating of our own, crumbling hearts.

Ikaria

Biography

Anita Sullivan tunes pianos in Eugene, Oregon, where she is known also as a poet, and founding member of Airlie Press, a women's poetry-publishing collective. Her first book *The Seventh Dragon: The Riddle of Equal Temperament* won the Western States Book Award for creative nonfiction in 1986, and for 11 years she was an occasional commentator on National Public Radio's "Performance Today." She lives in Eugene with her husband, piano historian Edwin Good, and is working on a novel that also takes place on Ikaria.

Books from Pearn and Associates, Inc.

Burning Daylight (Imprint):

Ikaria: A Love Odyssey on a Greek Island
By Anita Sullivan

I Look Around For My Life, Autobiography
By John Knoepfle

Goulash and Picking Pickles, Autobiography
By Louise Mae Hoffmann

Indian Paintbrush Poets (Imprint):

The U Book, Photos, Poems & Journal Notes from India
By Nathan Preston Pierce

Over the Rainbow (Imprint):

Another Chance, Young Adult Fiction
By Joe Naiman

Point Guard, Fiction
By Victor Pearn

Books may be ordered through amazon.com, barnesandnoble.com, your local bookstore, (Ingram Books) you may order for libraries through Baker and Taylor, and books may be ordered directly from the publisher at: happypoet@hotmail.com.

www.ingramcontent.com/pod-product-compliance
Lightning Source LLC
Chambersburg PA
CBHW021812220426
43662CB00006B/282